The 7 Secrets of Jazz &

Hammond Organ Bass Lines Demystified

Eddie Landsberg

DEDICATION

To all my students and supporters around the world, and in memory of some of my great mentors who are no longer with us: Big John Patton, Austin Mitchell, Bard Lancaster and Dottie Smith. Also in memory of the late great Bobby Watley and Charles Nesbitt.

CONTENTS

ACKNOWLEDGMENTS

In the course of this book you will learn how to construct, analyze and transcribe bass lines in the styles of the masters. While for copy write purposes the book does not contain note for note transcriptions, the lines in this book represent an amalgamation of the styles of almost all of the Jazz organ greats of the 50's and 60's including Wild Bill Davis, Jimmy Smith, Jack McDuffie, Richard Groove Holmes, Charles Earland, Larry Young, Don Patterson and many others.

Note on Notation in this Book: All bass lines in this book are written based on the key signature of C regardless the key of the tune. This is because most bass lines are not strictly diatonic or modal, therefore we are not focusing on one particular key center. I have also taken liberties with enharmonic voicings for ease of readings. For example if I'm playing C and its going to go up a half step then back down, in my opinion C C# C is easier to read that C Db C since sharp conveys the continued upward motion. On the other hand, if I'm going down from D to C, D Db C would be easier to read than D C# C...

PREFACE

I first decided that I wanted to play the Hammond Organ when I was in my late teens.

Although I had started listening to Jazz when I was around 14, within a short period of time I began listening to gospel, soul and Jazz, 1970's soul in particular, and the basic common denominator of all these great genres was the Hammond organ. Particular artists and groups included JB, The Ohio Players (their early stuff on Westbound), Black Heat, The Counts (*"It's What's Up Front That Counts"*/ Westbound) and Tower of Power. --Although I loved bebop, I didn't get the Jazz organ at first, with the exception of Charles Earland. I thought a lot of it was cheesy. But then I began living in Japan, and I started listening to Blue Note RARE GROOVE, stuff mostly out of print in the U.S. Reuben Wilson, Lou Donaldson, Grant Green, John Patton, Freddie Roach, Babyface Willette – and especially a track by Richard Groove Holmes called *"Onsaya Joy"*.

That got me...

After returning to the US, I began hanging out at places like SHOWMAN'S CAFE in Harlem NYC to see the masters at work, in particular Seleno Clarke, Bobby Forrester, Danny Mixon and Jimmy "The Preacher" Robinson.

At that point, I knew what I wanted to do, so I began my search for mentor. Unfortunately, at the time, the "second great wave" was yet to occur. Joey Defrancesco, Larry Goldings and Medeski Martin and Wood were rising in popularity, but basically Jazz organ music was still in recess, in part because whether or not the instrument itself was in or out of touch with the music of the era ("Fusion", the Fender Rhodes and later DX7 had put it into hibernation), the instrument itself, even other retro keyboards (Arps, Moogs and Clavs) were pretty much considered retro junk. --To that extent, I was lucky to get my first Hammond for $1000.

Over time, the battle of the "clones" began, starting with the XB-2... I'll be honest, the earliest of these instruments were great compared to what came before it, but most definitely NOT the real deal by any stretch of the imagination... but little by little, small improvements began to occur, in particular, the addition of waterfall keyes, and better chorus/vibrato (which beforehand was lousy to a fault!)

The first clone that really got me was the NORD ELECTRO. Within a few years the NORD C1 came out – and in my opinion it shattered the myth that nothing less than the real deal would do.

Meanwhile, I was well into my studies as a Jazz organist. At first, almost no teachers were available... and instructional material was limited. (Thumbs up to BT PRODUCTIONS who were among the first if not the first to put out useful Jazz organ instruction materials.)

Living in Philadelphia, I searched high and low at the time for a teacher. Players at clubs were rare, and those willing to teach were even rarer. --The internet was relatively new around then, and fortunately, thanks to Pete Fallico, an early online adapter and promoter/supporter of the Jazz organ medium I was able to hook up with the great Big John Patton after receiving help from Seleno Clarke and Shirley Scott, who was very ill at the time.

I remember the first time Pete told me that John would be willing to teach me. He warned me that he liked to freak people out, but that he was good people, and if I was patient and endured could learn the world from him. *It was true.*

The first time I met John was at his house in Montclair, NJ. I had travelled for 2 hours to get there and got there early, but the first time I met him he began yelling at me while I was still walking up the steps. Apparently, he thought I was late, and wasting my time and needed to stop *<expletive deleted>* and get on the organ... That was the beginning of a great mentorship which consisted of the master strutting and marching behind me, shouting orders (*"don't rush! Don't stop! Stop being a knucklehead!"*) and pulling my 12 bar bass line into order.

Studying with John was great. He had a distinct philosophy, even though he wasn't always so good at articulating things. I remember the first thing he taught me was I need to get my bass line solid. *"Once you get everything going down there, you don't need to do as much up top,"* he explained.

The idea that an organist had to be a good bass player, first and foremost was a key point in my training. I never thought of it like that. Prior, I thought an organist was a keyboardist who also played bass. But from the perspective of the masters I would come to study with, I learned the opposite, that in reality, a real Jazz organist is a bass player who happen to play keyboards. And think of it... *is it really possible to have a good Jazz band without a half way decent bass player?*

I was lucky to reach that route from the beginning. At that time many organists would want to play organ, but very little instructional material was available. They'd believe myths they heard here and there, and wind up going in the wrong direction. I remember, for example buying some vintage Jimmy Smith sheet music. The "transcription" consisted of right hand melody to BACK AT THE CHICKEN SHACK, left hand chords, and an *oompah-pah* bass line in the pedals. The draw bar settings were ridiculous. Basically *theatre organ* type stuff.

Then there would be players who had fantastic ears and would transcribe bass lines, and try to learn them note for note on the pedals. Some succeeded... and nothing is wrong with food pedal playing for those heading for that particular count and style (and who have the dexterity); however, the fact is that is not how Jimmy Smith, McDuff, Groove Holmes etc. usually played. To get the sound of a real string bass on the organ, basically this is what you do: You set the lower manual to 8x8000000... The position of the middle drawbar is debatable (I often have it to 0.) While you play the bass line in your left hand, you tap the pedal to add an extra pop and sometimes accent.

That time was the era before YOUTUBE. Today, hours and hours and hours of footage of Jimmy Smith can be seen – we know this today, but back then, pedal players would obstinately insist that you had to play the pedals to be a real Jazz organist. Some even knew the truth, but messed with people as sort of a cruel joke. Shirley Scott and Trudy Pitts, for example, both encouraged me to learn the pedals. (*I can play pedals, but I don't at all gigs.)

Long after Patton finally succeeded in getting my bass lines going I began to get some insight into the obsession with pedal playing so many organists had. It wasn't just a mis-perception, but based on the fact that back in the day so called "legit" organists were true foot pedal masters. (YouTube "Ethel Smith: *Tico! Tico!*) – so some who did play LH bass may have encountered "taunts" from legitimate players. *I experienced this once...*

I had put my first Jazz organ group together and the trumpet player introduced me to an old sax player who was touring with Illinois Jacquette at the time. He said he knew an organist who could really help me get my playing together. The fellow's name was Austin Mitchell, a player who Pete Fallico (the world's foremost Jazz organ authority) believed, based on thorough research, was long dead. He introduced me to Austin and Austin began hanging out at my house showing me stuff. --He was utterly shocked that I wasn't playing pedals and told me a story about being friends with Jimmy McGriff's father and him taking him to see his son play a concert. "We were up in the balcony and I looked down, and Jimmy wasn't even touching the pedals! I couldn't believe it!" he said in a voice of disapproval.

He also told me about a younger player (then in his 70's) who was able to play the new style (left hand bass) but also worked the pedals. The guy was Charles Nesbitt, a local circuit player who was indeed a master of the pedals and had a string bass kit added to his organ. One great memory I have of him was taking a solo in which he was squabbling, running bass (with his feet) and comping at the same time... NOT EASY!!! That said, these were older players... Charlie swung, Austin kinda reminded me of Bobby Short – definitely not a "groovy" type player, but a virtuousitic supper club type player, somewhat along the lines of the late great Jackie Davis. But I remember Charles telling me one time, "You don't have to BASH *all* the time!!!" – He was referring to modern 4 on the floor Charles Earland/Groove Holmes type playing, as opposed to more refined stuff.

To make a long story short, I began to progress... My lines weren't quite as smoothly flowing as I wanted them to be, and I remembered talking to Hank Marr who gave me the ultimate advice. "To be a good Jazz organist, all you need is a few good lines to get you up, and a few to get you down, then you can do anything!" I thought about that, and talked to John. I told him how much I dug Charles Earland's style of playing, and he began to show me some stuff (all of which appears in this book), and soon I was really flowing and at the point that I could get up and play gigs with real musicians in front of real people *How great it was!*

As for this book, part of the reason it came about was because I had so much trouble finding resources to learn Jazz, even before I began interested in the organ. And when I did find stuff, it just didn't seem to make sense, or be heading in the direction I wanted to go.

I remember my first lesson at Settlement Music School in Philadelphia. I was 14. The teacher pulled out a sheet to *Body and Soul* and began lecturing me on harmonic analysis and chord substitution theory. My homework assignment was to do a Harmonic Analysis of the tune... oh and while I was at it to memorize *all* 7 modes of the major scale in all 12 keys, all 4 inversions. *Umm... first lesson? How about a little music theory first?*

I had a similar experience at another school. The teacher pulled a sheet to *How High The Moon* and said to go home and learn a left hand walking bass line with right hand accompaniment using the tune's chord inversions.

These approaches to learning Jazz in themselves were not wrong, but you'd think they would have at least made an effort to assess what I did or didn't know rather than sitting down at the keyboard and whipping out the Rachmaninoff stuff. None checked, for example, if I knew my chords, basic music theory (essential for harmonic analysis), how modes worked and so on and so forth.

After years and years of struggling (in an era prior to GOOGLE where it became to learn anything imaginable simply by asking a search engine) I was almost ready to give up, when a teacher of mine began studying with Jimmy Amadea and recommended his book *"Harmonic Foundations for Jazz and Popular Music"*. Jimmy Amadea's methodological approach to chord construction really appealed to me. At the same time I was also studying Schillinger on my own. Bert Lignon's book on Linear Harmony also helped me out. Soon things began to come to together. Meanwhile, I was in the middle of my studies with John Patton, and there was a problem: John was a fantastic mentor and coach, but not always great at articulating himself. He's show me stuff, set the challenge, then send me home with the initiative to learn it, *or else*. Luckily, between my knowledge of Schilling's system of analysis, and Amadea's, I began figuring things out on my own, and soon was in the process of developing my own "school of the streets" system, one which had one objective: To summarize the rules of thumb that virtual all Jazz musicians know in the simplest language possible. It was around this time that I developed a theory: In order to become a good Jazz musician, its not just scales, chords and theory you need to know, rather you need to get in the head of really players and learn how they think. Ironically, around that time, a social anthropologist wrote a topic on that book, and I think it should be mandatory reading for all Jazz musicians. It was called *"Thinking In Jazz: The Art of Infinite Improvisation"* by Paul F Berliner. Read it, do lot's of listening and meanwhile...

Welcome to the *7 Secrets*.

Eddie Landsberg

<u>Preparing for the course</u>

The first step in learning any type of music is listening. There's really no way around it. Once the sounds are inside your head, getting them out is easy (or at least a lot easier) with a little training.

For this reason I recommend spending considerable time each day listening to key Jazz organ recordings. Before you even try to study how to play Jazz organ music, you want to have a firm idea in your head how it should sound, keeping in mind there is no one definitive right or wrong way to play Jazz, and eventually you have to either have your own idea how your instrument can sound, or at least be good enough to absorb the influence of other players convincingly.

My own concept is just as there are many different bass players, organists and schools and styles of Jazz, so to are there approaches you can take. This book aims at getting your feet wet, presenting the basics, and allowing you to then to take off in your own direction. If by chance you finish this book, begin studying Jimmy, Joey, Larry or whoever and conclude everything in this book was wrong, so long as I took you to the point that you could listen to them for yourself and reach conclusions as to whether I'm right or wrong, I've done my job.

Getting started: Can you hear the bass???

The ability to be able to hear and feel bass pulse sometimes requires developing... even some top level drummers I've worked with have told me that listening to Jazz organ bass takes a bit of getting used to.

Here's a recommended activity if you're not yet at the point where you can really hear what's going on in the bass.

Activity:

Boost the EQ to your sound system and begin listening to lot's of laid back swinging recordings.

Do this about 10-20 minutes a day while tapping your feet until you find yourself locking in with the pulse of the bass line.

Do not underrate the importance of this seemingly simple activity... You have to get to the point where the sound is really in you.

Suggested Preliminary Listening:

JIMMY SMITH: The Sermon

GROOVE HOLMES: Misty

CHARLES EARLAND: More Today Than Yesterday

Active Listening!!!

1) *Demonstrate ability to pat your foot 4/4 over a solidly swinging or grooving 4 beat tune for at least 6 choruses without falling out of sync.*

2) *Begin listening to the assigned pieces. Get them on your portable music device and spend a considerable about of time listening to them each day.*

3) *Listen to as many of the pioneering Jazz organists of the 50's, 60's and beyond. Think about who your favorites are and what you like about their style and want to study further.*

Assigned Listening

In my opinion, the handful of tunes below epitomize what swinging/grooving Jazz and groove feel is all about, but it is not meant to be conclusive. Feel free to modify, but remember, if you want to be taken seriously as a Jazz organist, you're going to need to prove that you've done your listening homework.

SWING

Charles Earland: More Today Than Yesterday

Groove Holmes: Misty

Jimmy Smith: The Sermon

Jack McDuff: A Real Goodun'

Larry Young: Softly as in a Morning Sunrise

Wild Bill Davis: April In Paris

Jimmy McGriff: All About My Girl

BOOGALOO/LATIN/FUNK

Lou Donaldson: Alligator Boogaloo

Groove Holmes: Song for My Father

Jack McDuff: Hot Barbeque

Jimmy Smith: The Cat

albums

*Jimmy Smith: Back At The Chicken Shack, The Sermon, Organ Grinder Swing, Midnight Special, The Dynamic Duo, Root Down (*and as many as possible!)*

*Lou Donalson: Natural Soul Alligator Boogaloo, Midnight Creeper (*and as many of his mid-late 60's organ combo albums as possible!)*

Jack McDuff: *The Honeydripper, LIVE, Hot Barbeque*

Wes Montgomery: The Wes Montgomery Trio – A Dynamic New Sound

Reuben Wilson: Love Bug

Big John Patton: Let' Em Roll, The Way I Feel, Along Came John

Dr. Lonnie Smith: Move Your Hand

*Jimmy McGriff: Greatest Hits (*too many to even begin naming!)*

Larry Young: Unity

Don Patterson: Hip Cake Walk

Pat Martino: El Hombre

Personal Faves

Freddie Roach: Good Move, Down To Earth

Wild Bill Davis: Live At Count Basie's, Midnight To Dawn

Babyface Willette: Stop and Listen, Face To Face

Joe Carroll: Man With a Happy Sound

Willis Jackson: (almost anything you can find, especially with Carl Wilson on organ and Pat Martino on guitar.)

NOTE ON BIAS OF SUGGESTED LISTENING TRACKS: I can imagine a few readers are thinking, "Why don't you simply compile these tunes and put them on a CD." --Unfortunately, to do this would mean that the book would have to cost a lot more. Today, most are available for barely a buck on iTunes, of course even better, the vast majority can be found on YOU TUBE. I also have to point out that this is not a definitive list of every Jazz organ recording you need to study and I haven't even concluded some of the "younger" players (its not that I don't respect them; rather, my aim is to start at the roots, so these are the players that most likely have influenced them. In the end, you need to do a lot of listening, not only to Jazz organ music, but Jazz and its related genres as well...)

Note on Ear Training:

Developing your ears can take time. As you learn to recognize common progressions, you'll find your hearing improving. You'll also learn that often what you can play is what you can hear, so the more stuff that you learn, the more you'll be able to hear.

As for starters, the following intervals are particularly important to nail from the get go...

1. Half steps *(thumb, thumb / pinky pinky / 5 4 / 1 2, 1 crossover up to 2)*

1. Fifths (up, down) *(5 2 up, 1 4 down)*

2. Fourths (up, down)

3. Octaves

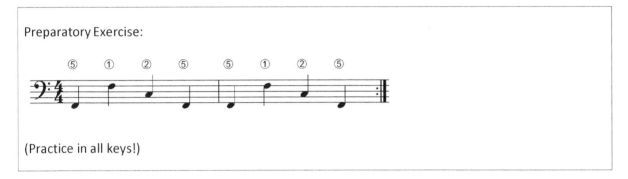

Preparatory Exercise:

(Practice in all keys!)

Ear Training Programs

A very good ear training app that I recommend is *RELATIVE PITCH*.

When possible, try to spend a bit of time each day learning to sing along with some of the lines from the recommended listening. If you can't carry a tune on the most basic level, I recommend *"The New Voice: How To Speak and Sing Properly"* by Alan Greene. Singing is the best way to connect yourself with your instrument, even if you have to intention of actually singing in front of other people. If you want to train your ears, **PRACTICE SINGING WHAT YOU PLAY.** Unless you born with it, trust me, it is the only effective way.

Right hand chords

Ideally speaking bass and chords should be learned together; however, in order to provide focus, this book centers entirely on LH bass. If you can play chords feel free to accompany yourself, but remember one key concept: In general, *right hand chord voicings must be rootless, otherwise you'll be competing with your own bass line.*

For starters, the basic voicing to use in most tunes are chords consisting of the third and seventh, with additional tones added up top. (3 5 7, 7 3 9, etc.)

For example if the change is C-7 to F7, your right hand chord need only be Bb Eb to A Eb...

This type of streamlined voicing is called a *shell voicing.*

You can then add other tones on top as needed... Bb Eb G to A Eb G...

Most of the time the key principal in developing your voicings (as will be the case with your basslines) is *economy of style,* meaning you don't want to have to move your hands around any more than you have to.

Please visit my website for further info on my chord construction courses.

note: Depending on your style of learning you might want to work on Chapter 2 before Chapter 1, only skimming Chapter 1 first. (*Chapter 1* covers the compositional aspects of a 12 bar blues bass line, while *Chapter 2* explains the fingering.) Do not proceed past Chapter *2*; however, until you can play the stock model bassline fluently.

1 BASIC CONCEPTS OF JAZZ ORGAN BASS PLAYING

Drawbar Settings & Basic Considerations: The basic drawbar setting for Jazz organ bass is 8?8000000. (The bass line is played in the lower manual.) The middle drawbar can be adjusted to taste. Now and then when I'm soloing, if I feel the bass is overwhelming my line, I occasionally knock in the third 8th a bit.

There is a common habit of Jazz organists taking the back off the Leslie. This is a great way to kill the bass, so I don't like it(!) Also, when possible, I like to disable the lower rotor to the Leslie.

There are numerous ways to enhance "bass weak" stock model organs ranging from direct line out/ compressed bass (when recording), to putting in a Trek II solid state amp. Sometimes weak bass can be the result of the tubes, other times the organ may need a bit of surgery. If playing a real Hammond, please refer to an experienced tech. On recording sessions, I almost always ask for a direct line out from the organ with isolated/compressed bass(!)

The Pedals: The focus of this book is left hand bass walking. You should; however, if possible tap the pedals when you play. This is a quick strike to almost any note that results in a popping or thud sound, not an actual tone. Tapping creates a feel of attack. If you don't attack, your lines are likely to sound syrupy at times. Please refer to vintage footage of Jimmy Smith on YOUTUBE playing mid to up-tempo swinging tunes to see the concept in action. *Notice how his foot is hovering over just a few notes even though the line clearly has more notes than his feet are actually playing(!)*

Ensemble considerations

Accompaniment: The drummer

When playing very orthodox Jazz organ swing or groove its important that the drummer has listened to a lot of Jazz organ music and knows certain techniques such as "feathering" (gently ghosting the kick) – Poor drumming can kill even the best of Jazz organ bass lines. In fact, it is said that there are Jazz organ drummers, and drummers that simply don't get it. While I think its important to avoid too many blanket statements, there is an issue of stylistic compatibility when playing any form of Jazz. In general, traditional Jazz organ drumming involves more "pocket" style playing and time keeping. If the drummer is too busy with accents on the kick, or going nutty on the cymbals, some tunes may not work. (This said, there are many different styles of Jazz organ playing.) Overall, when playing with less experienced drummers, always provide lot's of listening and when appropriate, point things out, for example, is the high hat to be played loud and crisp, or are more venturous Elvin Jones/Tony Williams like drumming styles that you wouldn't necessarily find on a Jimmy Smith/Jack McDuff type organ session acceptable. --If the drummer is not familiar with folks like Donald Bailey, Ben Dixon and Joe Dukes and there's not time to feed him with lot's of listening, you might refer to Miles Davis/*Kind of Blue* and Philly Joe Jones for starters – and, depending on your style ask them not to "comp" or fill too much (or even at all), and play with a strong 4 to the bar quarternote pulse. --As a final note, learning to play a bit of drums in the long term can actually help you become a much better communicator when it comes to dealing with drummers who don't quite get the sound at first.

Accompaniment: Guitar Both organ and guitar are choral instruments. This book is on bass walks not chords, but as a general rule you need to make sure your guitarist knows how to play **"shell voicings"** (rootless third and seventh voicings) and has listened to similar recordings as you. --*Bass clashing* is not acceptable, and while sometimes it can be a matter of tone, be careful if the guitarist is playing low roots, or lot's of low e-string and things like that. Whatever the case, watch out for two extremes: Guitarists who constantly clash with your chords, and guitarists who have a penchant for muddying up the bass. When possible, refer these players to classic Jazz organ recordings to listen to.

Jazz Organ Bass Lines: Basic Fingering Concept

Before we learn how to compose walking bass lines, we're going to jump right in and briefly analyze, then memorize a simple 4 beats to the bar bass line...

(At first I will present the line, after we analyze it, I will present the fingering.)

Before doing so, let's explore a basic approach to left hand bass walking: The key concept is this: **whenever possible try to play the roots and octaves with your pinky or thumb.** In my own style (which is used by many other, but not all organists), I usually allow my hand to hover around the root fifth and octave... If you watch videos of guys like Jimmy Smith and Joey DeFrancesco you'll find variations of this approach.

Basic hand positions:

pinky to index (root fifth) *ex. C G*

thumb down to fourth finger   (root fifth going down)

pinky index thumb (root fifth octave)

2 1 crossunder (chromatic lead-in to root, ex. Eb to D)
(!)**Practice playing root/fth patterns up and down in all keys using these basic hand positions.**

So, as you experiment with the bass line below, note that your pinky will play the F and Bb roots at the top of the first two bars. In the third your thumb will play the F... In the fourth your pinky the C and thumb the F (The passing tone will be played by your index finger.)

Note: *Anytime you learn a new shape or hand position, be sure to practice it in all keys until you can play the 1 or 2 bar pattern smoothly.*

Jazz Organ Bass Line Construction: Basic Concepts

(figure 1 -- See Chapter 2 for fingering)

Above we have a very basic 4 beats to the bar walking 12 bar bass line in F.

Rule #1 to understand is that basically speaking, **bass lines are FUNCTIONAL.** This is especially true if you want to be a Jimmy Smith style player. (Please refer to your listening assignment, **"The Sermon".**)

They outline the harmonic structure of the tune, and provide a basic rhythmic pulse.

To become good at playing bass lines you must understand the role of the bass player, then within that context have a system for cranking lines out on the spot that over tempo stability, and rhythmic as well as harmonic coherence. You must also understand that your first and foremost role in an ensemble is not to be a keyboardist who plays bass, or even an organist playing bass, but a bass player PERIOD... and in such, you must understand that you are foundation of the rhythm section.

To put things simply: **You must be a GREAT bass player overall.**

This said, we can ask the first question: How does **bass counterpoint** work?

It is simple... *The bass line outlines the harmonic structure of the tune.*

If bar 1 is an F7 chord and bar 2 Bb7, then we can guess the bass line is most likely going to go from F to Bb... Until we get into the realm of the fancy, its a no-brainer...

F ___ ___ ___ | Bb ___ ___ ___

Which leads to the question of how we fill in the blanks...

Amateurish players automatically assume that we're going to play some kind of scales or chords... but this misses a two key points:

1. *Bass lines are all about "forward momentum" (i.e. One note has to lead to the next.)*

2. *We always have to think how we're going to target the next chord.*

To do this, there are several basic strategies...

Strategy 1:

Most of the time you want to target chords from a half step above or below.

This means that in most cases the note that will be played before the Bb on the first beat of a Bb chord of any type will be A or B...

F_____A | Bb ____ ____ ____

Assignment 1:

Refer to *figure 1*. Circle the note before each chord change and note how the goal notes is targeted.

A half step above?   Half step below?

Getting off of notes

We've just learned how *to* get to notes, but what about off of notes?

Strategy 2:

Use fifths to maintain movement while prolonging the chords.

One basic (but not the only) strategy is to use the fifth as an extension tone...

(Please refer to the first bar of our 12 bar blues...)

We go F C F *(5 2 1 5 | 5)...*

C, the fifth, *prolongs* the F chord, B then *targets* the next chord...
F *C* F *B* | Bb

Root/Fifth/Octave movement played with pinky, index to thumb is a very basic left hand bass movement, therefore, it must be practiced smoothly in all keys!

Suggested Listening: John Patton's 1963 debut album, "Along Came John" (title track)

(!)It should go without saying, you need to know how to play your fifth intervals on the spot in all keys using pinky to the index as well as thumb to the fourth finger.

Important tip: Learn to Think Like A Bass Player!!!

It is natural for pianists to want to walk up and down scales; however, this not how bass players think. The goal of the bass player usually isn't to harmonize as a piano player or guitarist would. This would be getting in their way. Of course, this is most definitely not to say that the bass player should never play chord shapes or tones, but for the most part a good classic style walking bass line should not merely be outline of a bunch of chord shapes and scale patterns, otherwise, the bass player will be playing the exact same notes as the harmonic instruments in the band, leading to a flat one dimensional sound.

Example:

Bass --> F C F C

Guitar or organ comp --> Eb A

Played on keyboard, here's how it sounds: (F) Eb A C

The result is a nice open sound!

Note: Foldback Phobia

Some organists believe that they have to keep their bassline contained within a certain range of the lower lower manual. As a result of the fear of foldback and octaves, some players' lines become forcefully contained and don't swing. The fact is this... ROOT, FIFTH, OCTAVE is an essential bass line movement... although the core of your basslines will most likely be within the first and second octave in the lower manual, do not let "foldback phobia" inhibit your bassline!!!

Strategy 3:

Tonal jumps are ok, but use chromaticism to connect. (See analysis of figure 1, bar 2 below.)

Analysis of Figure 1 (con't)

Bar 2

Bb *D Eb* E

Here we skip a scale tone, then walk up chromatically to the IV chord.

Note: that the purpose of playing the third isn't to outline the chord, but to begin a chromatic walk up to the goal note, F...

Bb D <-- skip tone

D Eb E --> F <-- chromatic walk-up... E targets F from a half step below. The D targeted the E.

Bb D Eb E | F

Bar 3

In bar 3, we temporary stop the motion of the walk playing just the root, then the target tone. Good bass lines connect things smoothly, and although walking bass lines are supposed to do just that, walk, there is no reason we can't "ease on in" to a change.. so this bar offers a release in rhythmic tension and eases in to the next bar which serves the purpose of a lead in to the IV.

Bar 4

We already learned about targeting notes by half steps.

This is a typical *2 chord to the bar* ii V change... (*Most chord changes you will encounter will either be one chord to the bar or two to the bar changes... ex. C-7 | F7 vs. C-7 F7.)

Note how the chord notes are targeted from a half step above straight from the *lead in* to C, the *lead in* to F and the *lead in* to Bb.

Bar 5 and 6 *(*above)*

No comment should be needed... You already know this pattern!

Bb D Eb E | F Eb D (Db)

Remember, you can prolong a chord by using the fifth as the pedal point, so here, F is played under the second Bb.   Always remember → *FIFTHS PROLONG!!!*   This is a key bass walk principle.

You go up to the fifth (the note that prolongs the progression), then down, but at the last note be sure to target the note you want to get to.

Bars 7 + 8

Traditionally speaking the 7th and 8th bars return to the I chord, but in the modern era its a *transition* to the *run down* (the two bars before the *turnaround*.)

Hence we go from C C to Bb Bb to A to Eb D Ab to get to the G in the 9th bar.

Bars 9 + 10 --> The rundown

In an old blues, bar 9 would be a V chord and 10 would be IV... but in Jazz blues, a ii V progression is often used to smoothly transition into the turnaround. G→ C → F (as opposed to C to Bb.)

The purpose of a turnaround is to cycle back to the top. To do this, a I VI II V progression is called into play...

F7 D7 | G7 C7

ii | V | I VI | ii V ← *You need to know this progression in all keys!!!!*

INVERSIONS

Bass lines can always be inverted, so after you learn any given pattern, be sure to experiment with various inversions of the line...

You can also vary your lines by changing the direction of the tones you use to target. For example, in the first bar, F and Bb are targeted from a half step above, but in the second bar they are targeted from below.

You can also mix up the directions...

(!) **For all bass lines you learn in this book you can experiment with changing the direction of the target notes and experimenting with the pattern.**

Words of wisdom: I once asked Hank Marr what the secret to learning to walk LH bass. He told me a great player once told him you only need a few lines going up, and a few lines going down, then anything was possible!!! --This is true if you analyze the bass walking style of most great players!

2 FINGERING CONCEPTS

We've already learned some basic concepts of Jazz organ bass walking.   Let's see them in action...

Fingering (figure 1)

Memorize the pattern below in as many keys as possible. Fingering may vary...

Note on Fingering:

Always think about *economy and convenience of movement* when working out the fingering to a bass line. One common mistake organists make is fingering in wasteful ways that make fingers unavailable, as an example, if we finger from root to the fifth (ex. C to G) by using our pinky and thumb, the entire upper portion of the octave becomes inaccessible(!) On the other hand, using a Pinky/Index/Thumb pattern we can easily jump up to the top of the octave, or lower our hand down. In addition, many organists will use fingers other than their pinky and thumb to resolve to play the root: Be careful about this. In order to get your bass lines flowing its important to know where your fingers are at all time and be able to get them flowing. For this reason, its best to be consistent with your fingering. *When possible use identical fingering for identical patterns. (This is not a hard rule...an important rule in Jazz is, if it feels good and works right, do it!)*

Note: Any good musician should be able to keep solid time when required to do so... "groove" style players especially – BASS players most definitely. For this reason, a key point of focus when practicing these bass lines is TEMPO STABILITY, therefore you should practice along with CDs as much as possible Set as your main goal flow, consistency and tempo stability. Tempo stability, not SPEED should be your main focus.

Fingering Concepts

We can now examine our bass line with fingering. *Different players have different fingering systems, and a player's basic fingering and hand position can have a profound effect on his or her style of bass playing (as well as the stability of his or her line.)*   This is my own system which in part was handed down to me by Big John Patton.

Tip: Thanks to YOU TUBE you can get a great view of the master's in action. Some have been captured on video for posterity... others weren't. When possible, try to refer to footage of your favorite players then analyze their playing.   But remember, what works for one player may not always be appropriate for other players.

Analysis of fingering

Bar 1

Basic hand position. Keeping your pinky and thumb on the root and playing fifths with your index finger gets your hand in position to play some very convincing sounding bass lines, including, later on, various flips and embellishments that require mastery of root/fifth/octave movement.

(!) This pattern should be practiced in all keys.

Question: Why not play 4 to 5 for the last note?

Some players do this... but the 5 2 1 is a very stable bass pattern shape that later on allows for spontaneous flips and embellishments and you don't want to crunch your fingers up so they lose spontaneous access to the overtone notes, even of passing chords.

In the case of this progression B leads to Bb – So you could play a passing chord like B7 before Bb7... In that case, you might want to have quick access to the overtone notes...

Bar 2

This is a non-root/fifth/octave hand position. Notice how the second finger walks the thumb up to the goal note.

As a general rule, you don't want to have to change hand positions mid-walk. It can mess up your timing and make your walks unstable.

Another key principle of bass line fingering is that we want to play our goal notes with our thumb or pinky as much as possible... so here, the line is smoothly leading up to the thumb: *Practice playing it over and over in time until you get the flow!*

Bar 3

I'll admit this bar is a bit awkward, but it gets the hand ready for a very important transition... The ii V targeting the IV.

Bar 4

ii Vs are what Jazz is all about... and this is a very basic "two chords to the bar" two five line...

It should definitely be practiced in all keys with smooth 5 2 1 5 fingering.

Economy of Movement

Note: A key concept of keyboard performance is *economy of movement...*

Your hand should not be flopping all over the place, and your fingers should be ready to go where they need to go. This means your thumb is gracefully passing under your index finger in time to get to the F and while the F is being pressed your pinky is ready to do its job. Be careful about following orthodox key methods that require exaggerated hand movements, especially "wrist high" pecking techniques. Keep in mind that the organ, unlike the piano is not a percussive instrument: The basic feel is legato. If you watch video of most legendary players, you'll notice that even "high wrist "soloists tend to play a low, almost flat wrist in their left hand. -- An important element of piano technique is being able to strike keys with appropriate expression. With the organ, a lower wrist with more graceful hand movement may be advisable. Low wrist also allows a larger note span.

Bars 5 and 6

As mentioned, bars 5 and 6 are a very common walk, so you want to get the flow down in all keys.

Bar 7

As we discussed, some players might play lead-ins to the pinky with their fourth finger. Aside from the stretch being unnatural in many (but not all) cases, keep in mind that often bass articulation is usually based on a single attack pluck. Therefore, there is no need for notes to flow onto one another. The touch, while not quite staccato has to reflect a series of attacks, therefore playing the same note with the same finger is not necessarily a problem. It reflects the pluck, pluck, pluck articulation you'd get with a real bass, therefore, nothing is wrong with playing the half step lead in note to the goal note pinky to pinky.

This is that important ii V progression we discussed earlier. You should be able to play it on the spot without thinking any time you see a ii V progression. ii V progressions must be mastered in all keys!!!

Bar 9 and 10

Here we have the *rundown* leading to the *turn back*. Whereas the 7the bar represents a one bar walk on a ii V progression, the 9th and 10th bars represent a ii V progression played one chord to the bar. Make sure you can connect these two measures smoothly. Mastering it in all keys will give an almost unimaginable flow to your bass line over many common Jazz standards.

Note: I play Bb to B with my middle finger in order to avoid scrunching up my hand prior to having to go to the C. The result leads to a very smooth walk up to the F in the third bar...

Bar 11 and 12

And here we have the turnback, a pattern common in virtually any Jazz standard. This is another pattern that you must master in all keys and get smooth and flowing. Be sure to practice the two bars together and get a smooth flow as your hand creeps down back to the I.

You'll be using this pattern in a wide variety of tunes, and it is the basic progression of "rhythm changes" which after the blues is the most common song form in Jazz, therefore, memorizing your turn back in all keys can get you very far!

Note how in the first bar the use of my thumb gets my pinky ready to target the G...

And there we are... a 12 bar blues in F.

Important Point: Don't Underestimate the Importance of The Blues

Its said that a true professional Jazz musician needs to memorize about 100 tunes to really be called a true working professional. While this might sound like a formidable task its important to understand that most progressions that you'll find in all the other standards that you'll eventually find can be found in the blues (especially when you factor in various modifications to the form.) --Therefore, its essential to master the blues as an essential pallet in becoming an essential Jazz improviser. In addition to this, classic Jazz organ sessions tend to be heavy on blues changes – and virtually all Jazz greats recorded their own interpretations of the blues.

Some examples of Jimmy Smith below include *The Champ, The Sermon, Back At The Chicken Shack, Organ Grinder Swing, The Cat and Midnight Special.* At minimum, you must familiarize yourself with these numbers!!!

When I began studying with John Patton, he would not let me do anything other than practicing a stock model bass line that he taught me. It was taught by memory, and I was not allowed to stop, speed up or slow down. Sometimes he would stand behind me marching. This went on for almost 6 months and marked the transition between the point that I couldn't and could play a confident left hand swinging bass line. A key point to understand is that just about everything you learn from your 12 bar blues walk can and will be carried over to whatever else you do, whether its a standard or modern Jazz tune. Consider the blues a pallet for everything else... Therefore, you should be sure to memorize the line above (or one similar to it) and be sure to practice it for hours on end. (To this day, I almost always warm up on 12 bar blues in F.)

Once you get solid on the line, start listening to other 12 bar blues and little by little begin to branch out, ad lib and/or transcribe and modify the line. Your goal is to reach the point that the line transforms from a memorized pallet to genuinely in the moment evolving bass walk

REVIEW POINTS

There is no one right or wrong way to play a walking bass line and different players have different systems.

Economy and smoothness of movement; however, is important to consider.

When practicing, tempo stability is the first and foremost goal.

You can improve your dexterity, flow and vocabulary by practicing patterns in all keys.

According to Hank Marr, the secret of a good flowing bass line is having a few patterns to get you up, and a few to get you down.

3 HARMONIC ANALYSIS OF THE BLUES

Harmonic Analysis

In order to be an effective Jazz musician, ability to perform roman numeral analysis is an essential skill. Please refer to my *7 Secrets of Jazz and Soul* book if you need to dig down deeper into this.

Let's stop and analyze the harmonic movement of a 12 bar blues.

Overview of the Structure of a 12 Bar Blues

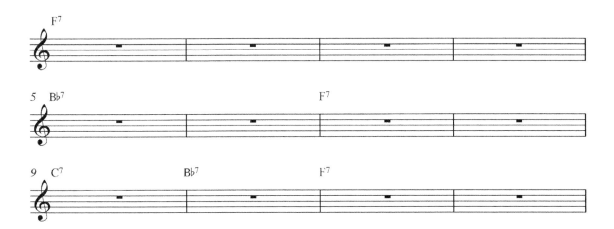

Figure 2

Before we move on, you should be able to play through the 12 bar blues in F above, either by playing the stock model line which you memorized in the previous chapter, or making a new one up.

Above are the basic changes to a "three chord blues" ...

It consists of 4 bars of a I7 chord... (with optional passing chords depending upon the tune.) The next measure is split between two bars of a IV7 and two bars of a I7 (but we learned, the I7 can be used as a transition to the rundown.)

The last measure consists of the rundown, which is either ii V to the I or V7 IV7 to the I...

(!)YOU MUST KNOW YOUR I IV and V chords in all keys!!! If you can't name them on the spot, you need to stop and learn them NOW!

I7	%	%	%
IV7	%	I7	%
V7	IV7	I7	%

So, here, via roman numeral analysis we can see the basic structure of a 12 bar blues. (Based on this info, can you name the chords to a 12 bar blues in C?

Another way to remember it is...

I7			
IV7		I7	
V7	IV7	I7	

To quickly figure out the chords in any key, simply write down the I IV and V in the key. (V is a whole step above IV.)

So let's say we're in the key of C, what are our three chords???

I7	IV7	V7

(!) Repeat: You must know the I IV and V chords in all keys before moving forward.

Now write them out in a 12 bar blues in C...

Answer: C7 | C7 | C7 | C7 |F7 | F7 | C7 | C7 |G7 | F7 | C7 | C7 |

Did you get it right?

Assignment:

Write out your 3 chord blues in the following keys as well especially G and Bb.

Listen to as many different blues as possible. Note whether they're V IV rundown or II V rundown variety of other and any special changes.

F.Y.I. Why are the I and IV chords in a blues usually dominant?

Depending on the tune, these aren't really dominant chord: they're major chords with altered 7ths. The tradition of tempering the 7th comes from old American vocal tradition – and is sometimes called a *barbershop chord* (from barbershop vocal harmony.) So keep in mind that the dominant chords in the 12 bar blues aren't necessarily dominant in the traditional sense of the word.

Practice Regiment Reviewed

If you want to become a good player, you need to get to the point where you can sit in with other musicians as soon as possible. Mastering your 12 bar blues in F, Bb, G and C, minor blues in C and rhythm changes in Bb plus few standards will definitely get you there.

Here is a basic practice regiment that will get you started:

1. **Memorize the line in this book until you can get it flowing and play it many choruses on end without stopping, stumbling or fluctuating tempo. (Consider playing along with a track like THE SERMON – you don't have to play the exact same notes as Jimmy Smith... just get it flowing.)**

2. **Get it down in other keys (Bb, G and C especially – Eb is also useful for bands that play SANDU. Db is the key DOODLIN' is usually played in. If you plan to play vocal sessions, go for all keys as soon as possible!)**

3. **Over time, try transcribing (or memorizing) walking 12 bar bass lines from various albums, even just a chorus... also listen to real bass players too. (Don't worry if you can't do it now. By the time you finish this book you're ability to hear the most commonly played walking bass patterns will be greatly improved.)**

4. **Be on the lookout for new rhythms and patterns when studying new tunes and try working them into your pre-existing lines.**

5. **Warm up every day by playing chorus after chorus of the blues for about 10, 15 or 20 minutes. Focus strongly on time keeping.**

In addition, as you listen to various recordings of famous 12 bar blues, be sure to note alternative changes that are played... chart them out if necessary, study the bass line and consider the variations that will result in your walk.

comping

In my next book, we'll learn about the art of chord accompaniment.

That said, let's take a brief peak ahead:

The first time I met John Patton one of the first things he told me was that if everything was happening down below (meaning in the bass), you don't have to play as much up top.

A good bass line can really open lot's of doors...

Take, for example the line we just learned: Let's couple it with some harmonizations that result naturally from the cadence of the line...

The bass line came from some relatively simple changes... 4 bars of the I chord, ii V leading to the IV, the transition to the run down, the run down and the turnaround, but look what we came up with along with way.

The use of chromaticism implies strong tri-tone as well as V I movement.

In the first bar, for example, we use F#7 to target F7, but actually its the same shape as C7#9 that we use in the next bar... On the other hand our bass line has substituted C for the F... yet when we targeted the C with Db, the V I cadence still works...

In the third bar, to get to C-7, we target it with Db7 or G7... The sudden presence of G7b13 after F7 seems unorthodox for a blues, yet it is logical (V I)...

Notice how melodic the line sounds...

The moral of the story here is that there is a lifetime of exploration that can be found in the blues, and solid, coherent bass counterpoint is where it all begins...

4 LATIN/BOOGALOO (1-5 OSTINATO)

Latin/Boogaloo/8 beat bass pattern

We're now going to learn how to pay a simplified "1 5" type bassline over a three chord blues.

As preparation, listen to the following tunes: *Horace Silver: Song For My Father; Lou Donaldson: Alligator Boogaloo; Lee Morgan: The Sidewinder*

Note: Above is an example of the basic pattern. *Please rely on listening, not reading to learn how it really sounds in all its variations and to get the swing. True Jazz feel can not be learend by reading notes of a sheet of paper!!!

Basically this is a pseudo latin type line. Very useful not only for boogaloo, but bossa as well.

The rest on the second space provides space for the high hat click. The fingering is 5 2.

The upbeat fifth creates a "forward momentum" style syncopation... In other words, the third beat starts on the and of the 2, but really belongs to the 3... +3.

In the ninth bar, the rhythm relaxes a bit. TENSION and RELEASE OF TENSION is an important thing to consider when playing basslines. This means you don't need to be all over the place all the time. Sometimes its important to relax a bit.

Toe Tapping

There are two ways to tap out this pattern in order to get your time stable.

Tapping on the 2 and 4, or tapping on all 4s, whatever the case, rhythms become weak when tempo is weak, since in essence all a rhythm is are "patterns over time"...

Therefore, its important to keep time.

Tip: Natural Time, "Nervous Time", Metronomic Time

Be careful about the difference between natural time, nervous time and metronomic time. Natural time is time similar to the beating of your heart... It may not be perfect, in fact, sometimes it breathes, but basically it is stable, and in fact to the casual toe tapping listener is indistinguishable for natural time.

Nervous time is what happens when musicians are too meticulous about time and as a result tend to push and pull the beat, while fighting to stay in time. In general, its not such a good thing.

Metronomic Time is time based on the strict click of a metronome. It is important to study and practice, but in reality music breathes, so musicians who can only play metronomic time wind up becoming disassociated from the natural flow of the rhythm section. *Perfectionism without connection is meaningless.*

The aim of most Jazz musicians should be relaxed, consistent, stable flowing but breathing natural time.

Suggested listening activity:

Simply listen to classic Jazz organ recordings and practice tapping your feet along to them until you find your timing falling in sync with the recordings.

Assignment:

1. *Take the 12 bar bass line below and write out in at least three keys.*

1. *Learn the bass pattern in all keys.*

2. *Rewrite the lines inverted (going down to the fifth instead of up) and practice playing them.*

Don't forget to pinpoint your I IV and V first and practice IN TIME.

Variation 2 – Boogaloo with pick-ups to the fifth...

I dotted the quarternote to emphasize that its a bit heavier than the other beats... but don't get too carried away... **RELAX!!!**

The rhythmic pulse of our previous bass line was similar to the half time samba of a simple bossa nova kick. Here we're going to double up the pulse a bit adding a little more motion...

So here we have a simplified boogaloo type bass line... (Have a listen to Reuben Wilson's BLUE MODE and Charles Earland's BLACK TALK albumsto get familiar with the sound.)

This is a 1-5 type bass line. I play the root pick up with my pinky.

Remember; however you decide to finger stable, consistent fingering leads to stable consistent time and *don't rush.*

TIP: Avoid 1-itis

Some "modern" players have a fear of playing the one too strongly.   In groove based Jazz; however, the beat and the pulse are very important, especially for a bass player, so be careful. Make sure you're feeling the beat and when its your job to play on the one... do it.

Tempo Stability

A good bass player must be a master time keeper...

Organists with a poor sense of tempo can really drive a good drummer nuts. --Poor tempo = poor drive, so if you aren't able to play in tempo, you might want to consider some metronomic practice over some of the exercises above.

Your goal is to get to the point that you can play root/fifth bass patterns with a relaxed yet stable feel.

One way to test yourself is to play a midi keyboard onto some music transcription software. Play the same pattern over and over again. --Do the notes look different every time, or is there rhythmic consistency? --Practice playing the same pattern over and over again until the transcription reflects consistent playing. Of course, this doesn't mean you have to play like a robot at all times. Its just an exercise and the purpose is to attain consistency in your playing.

Metronomic practice in 5 steps

1. Turn on the metronome.

1. Breathe easy.

2. Tap feet on the 2 and the 4.

3. Begin just by playing the one...

4. Once the one of each bar is in sync, begin playing +3. (Remember, the beat is toe down, the +s are toe up!)

5. Also, remember +3 has a short/long feel. Be careful that you're not playing two rushed/even dotted quarter notes.

Forward momentum feel:

The key point in syncopated music is that a phrase does not necessarily begin on the one... so being able to play onto the beat is very important. Mastering the "+3" is essential to mastering this skill.

Learning to feel the upbeat is an essential listening/feeling skill any Jazz musician needs to develop in order to swing.

Upbeat Feel Practice

Tap your feet counting 1 2 3 4 on toe down and + on toe up.

Practice only saying the + on the upbeat.

Next, say the + but snap your finger on the downbeat.

Say 1, snap your fingers on the two, then say + 3, then snap on the 4

Additional 1-5 Latin Type Patterns

Let's practice a "samba like" pattern with "+" onto the 1 and 3...

The two rests leave open the 2 and 4, beats that the drummer might click the high hat. This strengthens the groove. (Practice humming the line while snapping your finger on the rests.)

Back in the days when drummers strictly played the high hat on the 2 and 4 organists would traditionally sit up right next to the high hat in order to hear the click up the upbeat. This allowed for very type time keeping.

A great example of this style is listening to Jack Cuff's LIVE albums of the early to mid-60s, and various Jazz organ recordings with Ben Dixon on drums, not to mention Lou Donaldson's organ ensembles throughout the 1960's.

Suggested Listening:

The bossa nova wave in American Jazz to a large extent began with Getz/Gilberto's self titled album Getz/Gilberto (1963). Of course, not a Jazz organ album, but well worth listening to.

Lee Morgan: The Sidewinder (One of the famous boogaloos of the 1960's.)

John Patton: The Turnaround (*originally a Hank Mobley composition.)

Jack McDuff: Hot Barbeque (One of the most influential soul Jazz recordings of the 1960's.)

Jimmy Smith: The Cat (Note: JOS's most famous studio recording has a bass player, but live he usually played it without a bass player, and as an organist this is a tune that audience members hip to the Hammond sound may request, so its a good tune to learn!)

A key point is that there isn't just one type of Latin or boogaloo rhythm. There are many... so you have to listen and practice different variations each time you hear them. Often the notes will be surprisingly similar, but subtle variations in the syncopation will create entirely different grooves.

"UNBROKEN SPONTANEOUS FLOW"

A key goal to strive for when playing bass is achievement of a relaxed, smooth, unbroken spontaneous flow. To achieve this, its a good idea to memorize a few stock model bass lines and get them flowing. When you practice set a goal, for example 12 continuous choruses. You must then be able to play the line without stopping or getting lost for 12 choruses straight.

As you play your lines, you can try to add stuff in and mix up your lines, incorporating as many ideas as come to mind.

To check out the consistency of your line you can record yourself and time the first few choruses then the last few. If you find yourself speeding up dramatically, you may want to practice along with some of your favorite albums.

some additional tunes to learn:

By now, you should have your basic blues form memorized.   Let's apply these concepts to some additional tunes...

Song for My Father

A good tune to begin working on at this point is Horace Silver's SONG FOR MY FATHER. It is a groovy bossa nova who's A section has the following changes:

F-7 | F-7 | Eb7 | Eb7 |

Db7 | C7 | F-7 | F-7 |

The bridge is:

Eb7 | Eb7 | F-7 | F-7 |

Eb7 Db7 | C7 | F-7 | F-7 |

It should be pretty easy to remember: Just remember the chord decension... F Eb Db C, then the bridge kinda turns things around Eb F, then Eb down to C7 and F again...

Work on it without looking, then try playing along with some recordings.

Suggested Listening:

Horace Silver: Song For My Father

Groove Holmes: Song For My Father

We'll learn the bridge in the next chapter.

The Girl From Ipanema

This bossa is commonly called at most standards sessions, so its good to know. The bridge is also a great test the fluidity of your 1 5 movement.

Don't write it out. Sit down and using the same rhythm from the A section of *Song For My Father* try to play through it on the spot. If you find yourself stumbling, especially when you get to the bridge, you need to practice your 5 2 fingering root/fifth patterns.

Here are the changes:

The A section is very similar to *"Take The A Train"*, only its in F...

Fmaj7 | Fmaj7 | G7 | G7 |

G-7 | Gb7 | F7 | F7 |

The bridge gets a bit goofy... but its a good test to see if you truly have your 1 5 patterns down!

Gbmaj7 | Gbmaj7 | B7 | B7 |

F#-7 | F#-7 | D7 | D7 |

G-7 | G-7 | Eb7 | Eb7 |

A-7 | D7b9 | G-7 | C7b9 |

Sunny

This is a really fun tune to play, and easy to memorize.

The changes are:

A- | C7 | Fmaj | B- E7 |

A- | C7 | Fmaj | B- E7 |

A- | G- C7 | Fmaj | Bb7 |

B-7 | E7 | A- | E7#9 |

(So basically its the same progression over and over with a few tweaks here and there...

There are so many great versions of this tune... though, come to think of it, as often as I've heard it at organ sessions, I can't think of a definitive organ version.

Among some of my favorite versions are Stanley Turrentine's, Les McCann and George Benson's!

Here's my version which includes a hybrid of some of the bass line strategies we've learned so far...

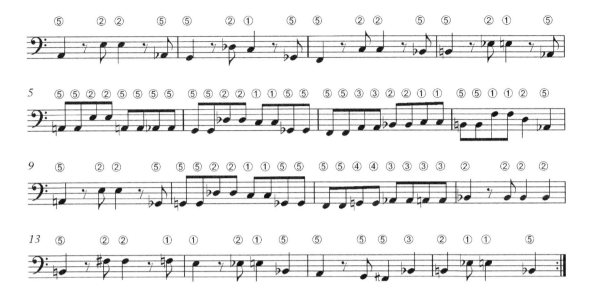

comment:

Do you agree with the choice of fingerings on this bass line? Note that while in the academic world we can change the fingerings to suit the bass line, usually in the real world, we're going to work with the notes that fit our hand position. Can you think of ways of changing the fingering or notes on this bass line to make it flow better?

Note: I've also included an 8 to the bar soul music influenced walk. You can also do broken octaves over this type of walk.

Watermellon Man

Watermellon Man (and Cantaloupe Island) are among the most commonly called tunes at Jazz sessions. WATERMELLON is a 16 bar blues. The *rundown* (V to the IV) repeats itself 3 times before a break.
--Listen and learn: (*Herebie Hancock: Taking Off 1962*)

Cantaloupe Island

Here's yet one more tune that will get you very far with a simple 1-5 type bass line. Its also commonly called at many jam sessions.

F-7 | F-7 | F-7 | F-7 |

Db7 | Db7 | Db7 | Db7 |

D-11 | D-11 | D-11 | D-11 |

F-7 | F-7 | F-7 | F-7 |

Have a listen to the original on *Empyrean Isles.*

How would you modify the syncopation and flow of the bass line to better fit in with groove?

How To Stop Getting Lost

Do you find yourself frequently getting lost in model tunes that don't have lot's of changes?

If this is a problem you might want to practice counting.

In the case of Cantaloupe Island you can count BARS, not beats...

If you were counting beats and bars together, you'd go...

1 2 3 4 | *2* 3 4 | *3* 2 3 4 | *4* 2 3 4 | etc.

You also have the option of counting the beats between the beats, for example..

1 + 2 + 3 + 4 + | 2 + 2 + 3 + 4 + | 3 + 2 + 3 + 4 + | 4 + 2 + 3 + 4 + (etc.)

The tune is pretty hypnotic and straightforward, but all that counting might be a bit verbose, so after initially practicing by counting the beats, graduate to just counting the bars and key beats. With practice you might reach the point where you're just feeling the + beats.

Try it by listening to the tune, tapping your feet with toe down on the beat, and toe up on the upbeats, saying the + beat out loud. Next, try to get to the point where you can just FEEL the upbeats, are tapping the downbeats but aren't so hung up on them... and at the same time are counting bars... Remember though, the tune has only 4 changes, so you might want to count to 4 then start over all four times.

5 BUMPS, FLIPS AND EMBELLISHMENTS

As mentioned earlier, for the most part, Jazz organ bass lines are functional; however, different organists have different styles and tricks that they pull out, some regularly, some on occasion. Its a good idea to listen to as many masters of B3 as possible, then decide what elements of their playing you find best for what you do. There is no one right or wrong way to play. That said, this chapter will get you away from strict 4 to the bar playing and help you open up your line.

Half Time Walk / Tri-Tone Substitution via Chromaticism

Let's return to our swinging 12 bar blues bassline briefly...

Here's a walk up with an almost half time feel in the root movement. (You can attach it to the bass line we learned in the second chapter.

The first two bars should make sense, but what about the third bar? It uses two important bass line concepts: *Neighboring Tone Chromatic Prolongation* and *Pedal Tone Prolongation.*

<u>Neighboring Tone Chromatic Prolongation</u>

Earlier, we learned that you can extend a chord by going to the fifth. Another option is going to the note a half step above or below it then back. *After that you need to target the tone you want to go to...* (See figure 2.)

Pedal Tone Prolongation

The "C" in the line above represents the C not of a C major, minor or dominant chord, but simply C in the bass under F (a.k.a. F/C) --however, we want to go to C in the next bar anyway.

--Finally, the purpose of bar 4 is to target bar 5 with a ii V progression in order to ensure a smooth progression to the IV. This device is called *ii V targeting*.

Normally the movement would by C-7 F7 | Bb7, but F has been replaced by its tritone substitute B7.

Here is the basic rule: **To go from ii to V you can play ii bii7 instead...** (This is a type of tritone substitute.)

Let me repeat this...

Tritone Substitution:

Bass lines can be chromatisized by replacing the V with the note a half step below the II...

ie D-7 G7 | C-7 F7   D-7 Db7 | C-7 B7 |

Let's take **CONFIRMATION** or **BLUES FOR ALICE**, for example... (*Please listen to a few versions first!!!*)

Here are the basic changes:

Fmaj7 | E-7 A7 | D-7 G7 | C-7 F7 | Bb7...

Here is the line with the conventional ii V changes...

And here's the same line chromatisized...

But we can also add motion within the chromaticism... notice how the C prolongs the F in the first bar...

And here is the same line rhythmically embellished...

Chromatic Neighboring Tone Prolongation

Below we have an example of chromatic neighboring tone prolongation as applied to a 12 bar blues. Once you have the basic concept and feel down you can pretty much apply it to any standard to create an instant driving bass line on the spot.

A key concept is that tones are *prolonged* as well as *targeted* via neighboring chromatics. Note the consistent 2 1 fingering...

<u>Triplets and Flips</u>

Now we return to *Confirmation*...

Above, we saw a number of ways of swinging our bass lines. In the first bar rather than playing a straight 4/4 pattern, there is what I like to call a "triplet bump"...

It goes 1 +2 3 4... much like a typical Jazz ride pattern on the drum kit.

Its important not to think of this line as 1 + 2 3 4 or even 1+ 2 3 4... The triplet note belongs to the second beat not the first, so really it is the + swinging on to the two...   1 +2 3 4

Syncopation = Jazz, always remember this!!!

The feel is very subtle, but it is the epitome of what Jazz is all about. If a tune is said to be swinging in the traditional sense of the word, these "upbeats" between the beats must constantly be felt.

Musicians who can't swing often do so due to a tendency to think in straight 8ths, rather than swung eighths.... .

Here is an example what the line would sound like if played by a player who can't swing.

To compensate for the lack of swing, players will simply try to play in fast tempos. I call this the "electric bass player's syndrome" as its most common with players who switch from acoustic to electric bass.

In order to get away from heavy, mechanical, non-swinging feels (*or should I say *lack of* feel) learning to play with both forward momentum and triplet feel is essential.

Here for example is the sound of quarter notes, eighth and triplets...

Watch what happens when we add rests in between the notes...

(Be sure to continue tapping and counting so the notes retain their proper duration... and play this exercise over and over until you can really feel the difference in the durations.)

In Jazz, the duration of eighth notes are not necessarily full eighths, but more a long-short alteration... (Actually, short/long if we consider the syncopation *onto* the beat.)

The basic pulse is more like this:

The logic of this feel is sometimes described mathematically, but the truth is that it is a feel that requires an intuitive understanding. Once the pulse is part of your style, it'll be ever-present in your playing whether or not you're thinking about it. This is what it means to swing.

Until it gets there, one trick is to get away from the "1ee+ee" and 1 + 2 + 3 + 4 type counting you probably learned in school and try to feel the basic count as thus...

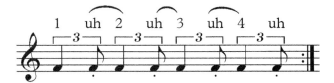

Likewise, even when you see quarter notes, count them as triplet...

The implication of this is that you can practice modifying the duration of the quarter notes to enhance the feel of the tune...

For example...

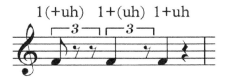

All three of these notes might appear on paper as quarter notes in Jazz, but the articulation of each is different. To practice, count 1+uh 2+uh 3+uh 4+uh, but only play the beat not in parenthesis. After practicing the exercise over and over, try to play through a major scale using the different articulations as well as combinations of them.

If you're having trouble feeling or playing swing beats, I'd strongly suggest listening to Art Blakey's **MOANIN'** over and over again as well as Jimmy Smith's **Back At The Chicken Shack** -- Don't listen to the bass player, rather the pattern of the cymbals, and feel the "shuffle" while tapping your feet.

Important Point: Beyond the music that's written on paper, different styles of Jazz have different types of "swing" or "pulses". As you listen to many different recordings and style of music, see if you can observe underlying feel that epitomize the playing of various players. Then compare, for example Charles Earland to Groove Holmes and Larry Young: How would you sum up the key differences in their signature bass lines and what would you do to capture them?

ANALYSIS:

Bar 1 - 2

The first bar is an F major chord leading in to E-7(2ND bar) from pick-up Eb.

To prolong the F there is a flip consisting of Root Five to the octave then back down to the fifth.

This is a very common flip pattern and should be practiced in **all** keys.

The second bar uses chromatic lead-ins to target a the E-7b5 A7 ii V progression, then targets the D of the next bar from a half step above.

Bar 3

This has a groovy stop and go feel by repeating the same note twice rather than holding it for the full quarter.   It must be done with that punchy short-long feel.

Jack McDuff and Groove Holmes were masters of this feel, so I recommend listening to them day and night.

Bar 4

Here we have another bump, but this time root to the fifth.

The fifth resolves down a half step, because it needs to get to the V of the ii.

C-7 --> F7

Key Point:

Great Jazz organ bass lines can be 4 beats to the bar, and no doubt the basic pulse should have a strong 4/4 feel, but via triplet subdivision, a wide variety of polyrhythmic feels that enhance the swing can be created.

Pick-up onto the flip

Back to **Confirmation**, we can see a pick-up onto the flip... (uh1 +2 3 4)

The most common mistake bass players make is rushing the pick-up.

A good count-off should resolve this problem*

1 – 2 – +1 2 3 4 + (Remember, the pick-up comes in on the +.)

Here we have an exercise that can be practiced in all keys to improve your ability to play onto the beat:

It should be practiced with a metronome...

How To Count Off A Tune

The best way to become good at playing pick-ups is learning how to properly count of a tune.

Here are the basic steps to counting off a typical swing based tune...

1. Begin singing the melody in your head.

2. While doing so start tapping your feet to keep time.

3. Count 1 – 2 – | 1 2 3 4 while snapping your fingers on the 2 and 4.

4. Stop the count before the pick-up comes in.

You can catch the swing if you want by counting uh1 – 2 uh | 1 2 3...

Key point:

We need to move away from feeling the "1" as the first beat. When we're swinging, everything is onto the 1, so we really need to feel the pick-up!!!

Chromatic Double Pick-up onto the flip

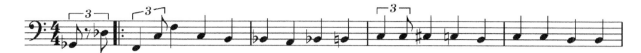

Let's return to our 12 bar blues...
Here, the changes are F7 | Bb7 | F/C | C-7 B7 |

Analysis

pick-up

Previously, we used a half step to target the F of the first bar.

Here, we also use a half step, but also go up to the prolonging fifth. (The pattern can also be played in reverse. Bb Eb onto D.)

Fingering is very important on this. As a general rule, its a good idea to try to keep similar fingerings for similar shapes. This will enhance the rhythmic consistency. Hence 5 2 to 5 2 in the first bar is the probably best. (*or 2 5 to 5 2 if played in reverse.)

Rhythm: The rhythm in the pick-up is slightly different from the rhythm in the first bar. In comparison, the first 1 5 pattern has more drag. Again, don't rely on printed music to get the feel... *always go for feel over print.*

The key point to remember is that the lead in 1 5 pattern in the first bar needs to smoothly connect with the second beat. We don't want to break the flow from the pick-up to the second. Everything has to consistently flow to the point that it needs to go.

Bars 2-5

The chromaticism in bars 2, 3 and 4 (leading into 5) create a teetering effect, smoothly leading the line to the IV chord (Bb) in the fifth bar.

We can contrast this with other strategies including straight walks, as well as "ii V" type walk downs, such as in *BLUES FOR ALICE.*

Contrast is a very useful way to keep bass lines interesting – so we can use mostly chromatic movement in the first measure, then when we get to the fourth do a strong walk. This will create the impression of release, as well as an energy build as we lead into the *rundown.*

More Flips

This bass line has numerous flips and bumps...

How many flip patterns can you find?

(!) memorize the line...

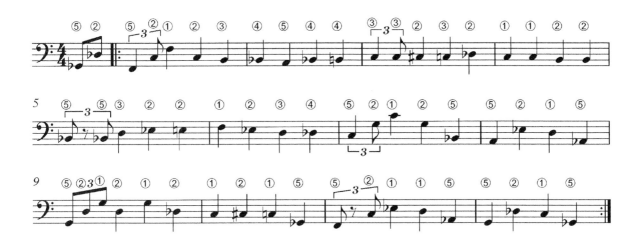

Analysis:

Bar 1

Bar 1 is a simple prolongation device...

root to the fifth to the octave.

The remainder of the bar is targeting the Bb in the next bar.

Bar 3

This is a simple "bump"... in addition, the chromatic neighboring tone a half step above is used as a prolongation device. This is a good pattern to practice in all keys.

Bar 5

Yet another bump. These bumps are useful at the start of a new "phrase", or even in the middle, but be careful not to overdo them or they'll sound messy and haphazard.

Bar 7

Normally the 7th and 8th bars are a return to the I, here, the fifth of the one is used to ease on down to a ii | V walk up to the *turnaround* in the last two bars... F7/C | A7 D7 | ...to G..

Bar 9 + 10

Here we have a completely new type of flip. Practice it in all keys!!!

Its an actually Root/Fifth/Octave triplet...

The entire bar prolongs the G chord until the very last note, which targets the "C" which is prolonged by going to the neighboring chromatic tone then back.

Bar 11 + 12

Our turnaround prolongs the F, but shoots up to the chromatic lead in to the VI...

Syncopation Practice

ETUDE #1

Here we have an exercise that can be practiced in all keys. It is a series of "swingersizes" that I've developed over the years for my students... Once you master the pattern in all keys you'll have your basic flip hand positions down, as well as some of the basic rhythms and syncopations.

ETUDE #2

Playing lines with syncopated pick-ups can be difficult, so here's another exercise that can be practiced in all keys...

The rhythm is... uh1+uh (2) uh3+uh (4)... (*open snap beats in parenthesis.)

Understand that the two and the four represent the click of the high hat... In your mind, the lick should be answering the click of the high hat.

So you have...

uh1+uh (click) uh2+uh (click) uh1+uh (click) uh2+uh (click)

Your foot should be solidly tapping on all four beats...

Practice this *swingersize* over and over with 2 5 2 1 fingering until you can play it many times over and over without breaking the rhythm...

ETUDE #3

Learning to swing 8th notes is essential to be able to play with a groovy feel... Bass lines can be played with straight 4 feel, but they're not going to swing as hard and lack the a true sense of *forward momentum.*

Forward Momentum

This is the sense that the music is constantly moving forward hence the reason bass lines are often called "walking bass". There are a number of ways that it can be achieved. One is simply by having a constant driving well connected 4/4 pulse. Yet another is swinging onto notes. In the exercises above, two weaker notes swing onto "2", which in Jazz is the emphasized beat. (The 1 is relatively week, the two and four are strong.)

Understanding the importance of the 2 and 4 and lightening up the 1 and 3 are essential.

It is also important to distinguish between the downbeat and the upbeat.

Here we have an exercise that can help you develop this feel...

Its a very basic shuffle pattern.. I've dotted the quarter notes so they're not played too heavy but accented a bit... The most important points are that they beat is uh1 uh2 uh3 uh4... pick-up ONTO the beat...

Played properly the beat should sound a bit like a train or the gallop of a horse, and remember, you're playing the short off beat note onto the quarter, not visa versa.

Suggested Listening: *Honky Tank (Bill Dogget), Funky Mamma (Lou Donaldson)*

Assignment:

Now, please listen to Jimmy Smith's ***BACK AT THE CHICKEN SHACK***.

What key is it in?

What are the changes Jimmy Smith is playing?

Based on the bass line strategies you've learned in this book so far, transcribe the choruses of the bass line behind the solo... What is the basic pattern Jimmy is playing? (You'll notice he breaks it quite a bit... but you should be able to hear it?)

Listen to Jimmy's bass line behind the solos... How many basic patterns can you hear?

Transcribe at least one or two choruses.

Additional Prolongation Pattern

Try out the line above using 5 2 1 type fingering.

Using some of the methods we've already learned, let's find ways to embellish the line...

This is almost the exact same line as the one above, and it demonstrates the logic of 5 2 1 fingering:

1. The 2 is emphasized, being the heaviest beat in most bars... All beats are leading onto it.

2. The four leads onto the one, but the one leads onto the 2, hence the line is constantly moving forward.

If you refer back to the very first bass line in this book, you will see that it is possible to swing creating a straight 4 beat pulse, but its important to be able feel the beats between the beats and add to them when necessary.

Note: I added a bit of extra weight to the first beat of the first bar. Emphasizing the first beat of the first bar enhances the phrasing of the bass line. It is subtle, but effective.

Syncopation Applied for Freer Feel

release of tension/Song for My Father (Bridge)

We can alter the rhythm in the bridge of tunes to add contrast and keep the focus of the listener.

Here, the bass has a more open and free flowing feel.

In the first flip variation, the line fires up to the ninth with a broken triplet. The rhythm varies over the F-7 chord with a straight triplet. There is then a walk down, a break in the 6th and return to the ostinato like line.

Although the tune has a groovy bossa feel, swung pick-ups keep us in the realm of Jazz.

Tritone Chromatisation Review:

A good tune to practice swinging and chromatisizing ii V progressions on is **HAVE YOU MET MISS JONES.**

The chord progression to the A section is quite simple...

Its written in most fake books as...

Fmaj | F#dim7 | G-7 | C7 |

A-7 | D-7 | G-7 | C7 | *(leading back to the top)*...

But actually F#dim7 is a sub for a VI chord (D7b9), and we can enhance the flow of the song by playing it thusly:

Fmaj | A-7 D7 | G-7 | C7 |

A-7 | D-7 | G-7 | C7 |

Performing a roman numeral analysis on the tune, it looks like this: I

| iii VI | ii | V | iii | vi | ii V

Pretty simple, right???

Listen to some recordings of the tune. Next, try making up a simple walking bass line without any reading or writing.

Now, here's where things get fun:

The bridge goes to the IV... (This should not be surprising as the IV serves as a temporary key center in many tunes.) However, the changes are revolutionary, as it consists of ii V progressions modulating down by major thirds. (Fast forward 20 years and think **GIANT STEPS**.)

As written in many fake books, it goes like this:

Bbmaj | Ab-7 Db7 | Gbmaj7 | E-7 A7 |

Dmaj7 | Ab-7 Db7 | Gbmaj7 | G-7 C7 | *(back to the third A section.)*

You can practice this unusual progression in all keys by first identifying the IV in the key center, then pinpointing the three major chords...

For example, let's say we're doing it in the key of C. The bridge is in F, so we'd have to do F Db A...

And don't forget, it goes down twice, then repeats the middle chord, then heads back home...

Now, look what happens when we engage in a little tritone substitution...

Bbmaj7	Ab-7 G7	Gb maj	E-7 Eb7
Dmaj7	Ab-7 G7	Gbmaj	C7alt

The line is quite chromatic...

Bb Ab G B E Eb D...

But we can go further... (note: These are my subs, not the right or wrong way to play the tune...)

Bbmaj7 A7	Ab-7 G7	Gbmaj F7	E-7 Eb7
Dmaj	Ab-7 G7	Gbmaj	G-7 C7

Under a bass line like this, the accompanies could still comp conventional changes (ignoring the passing subdominant chords) and the bass line would have a very driving feel.

Pedal Tone Embellishment

One other powerful way a song can be embellished is by the bass player hanging on the pedal points...

For example, to an 8 bar introduction to Miss Jones can be created by the bass hang on pedal point C (the fifth of the key) while the regular changes to the A section are playing.

So the bass might go like this:

Or even something like this...

The cymbals won't be riding – instead there will be a freer, more open feel – however, the chords will still be the same...

C	E G A C
C	F# C F
C	F B E
C	E Bb D#

On the other hand the individual chords can also be sustained by placing their roots a fifth up and suspending the walk...

Bbmajor/F

Ab-7/Db

Db7/Db

Gbmaj/Db

E-7/A

A7/A

Dmaj/A

One of the first tunes to be written embodying Sus Chords through an entire chorus is Herbie Hancock's MAIDEN VOYAGE... prior to this you will hear plenty of tunes where to build energy through a certain section of a tune the bass player stops walking and just hangs on a pedal point.

When using this type of device there are two things to keep in mind – First, you might want to embellish it by holding down the (proper note) on the pedals, second, don't overdo it. If the purpose is to build tension, sometimes one section is enough, then let go and start swinging like there's no tomorrow...

Assignment: *Write out the changes to a favorite tune. Above the chords, experiment with various pedal point ideas over various sections.*

Write out pedal point intros to some of your favorite tunes. Don't be afraid to experiment with unorthodox tones as well.

6 MINOR BLUES AND MINOR KEY TUNES

Minor Blues

Blues, Minor Blues and Rhythm Changes are essential vehicles that can help get you up and playing at most straight ahead jam sessions. They're also useful because they teach you to pinpoint the I IV and V in various key centers, as well as connect your changes.

While the bebop era was heavy in major key blues, the hard bop era saw a greater embracement of minor blues like forms.

Let's learn to play a basic minor blues...

The basic form of a minor blues is as follows:

I-7	I-7	I-7	I-7
IV-7	IV-7	I-7	I-7
bVI7	V7	I-7	I-7

*Note on the Run Down

Besides the chords being minor, a key difference between the major and minor blues is that the rundown consists of bVI7 to the V as opposed the V to the IV; however, it should not be too surprising when you realize that Ab7 is merely the tritone of D7.

(In order to be able to play the minor blues, as well as minor blues influenced tunes efficiently you should be able to pinpoint the bVI7 to V progressions in all keys!)

Using ii V progressions for the purpose of harmonic prolongation

Keep in mind that ii V progressions can be used to prolong the one, so we can rewrite the tune with a ii V in the second bar. Actually, since its a minor blues, ii-7b5 V7(b9) would be more appropriate.

C-7	C-7	C-7	C-7 (to F)

Becomes...

C-7	D-7b5 G7	C-7	G- C7

In addition, we can target the IV (F-7) with a ii V progression leading to it.

In the 6th bar, we can also retarget the I-7, then in the 8th we can target the VI7, then end with a turnback... Here is how it would look:

C-7	D-7b5 G7b9	C-7	G-7 C7
F-7	D-7b5 G7b9	C-7	Bb7 Eb7
Ab7	G7	C-7	D-7b5 G7b9

Key point: Use ii V progressions to prolong or target changes...

Reharmonization for Chromatic Root Movement

Now watch what happens if we add the V to the 7th bar, then chromaticise the changes from the 4th bar, using Eb to transition to D-7b5...

C-7	D-7b5 G7b9	C-7	G-7 C7
F-7	D-7b5 G7b9	C-7 *F7*	Bb7 Eb7
Ab7	G7	C-7	D-7b5 G7b9

Becomes...

C-7	D-7b5 G7b9	C-7	G-7 C7
F-7 F-7/Eb	D-7b5 Db7	C-7 B7	Bb7 A7
Ab7	G7	C-7	D-7b5 G7b9

G-7 Gb7 | F-7 Eb7 | D-7b5 Db7 | C-7 B7 | Bb7 A7 | Ab7 | G7....

The line (unembellished) would look like this...

G Gb Gb | F F Eb Eb | D D Db Db | C C B B | Bb Bb A A | Ab Ab Ab Ab | G G G G...

Your challenge: Write out a 12 bar minor blues based on these changes:

But, we can also take the changes to this line and smooth them out even more:

C-7	D-7 G7	C-7	G-7 C7
F-7 F-7/Eb	D-7 G7	C-7 F7	Bb7 Eb7
Ab7	G7	C-7	D-7 G7

Here, a gradual descent begins from the 4th bar...

			G Gb
F Eb	D Db	C B	Bb A
Ab	G		

Once we get the flow of this walk down under our fingers, playing through the minor blues is easy, since all else it is a C- turn back...

One of my all time favorite minor blues is **WHEN MALINDY SINGS** from Freddie Roach's GOOD MOVE ... Have a listen and see if you can catch the form! An even more famous version of an altered minor blues is Oliver Nelson's **STOLEN MOMENT**S from **BLUES AND THE ABSTRACT TRUTH**. Have a listen!

Eddie's Delight

But the minor blues can also be excellent vehicles for departure.

Here are the changes to my original composition, *Eddie's Delight.* (*Check out my website!)

G-7	A-7 D7#9	G-7	D-7 G7b9
C-7	A-7b5 D7b9	G-7	C-7 F7b9
Bb-7 Eb7b9	A-7b5 D7#9	G-7	Ab13

Can you see where the linear decent begins? You might be surprised.

Actually, there are two extended descents...

			D Db
C B*	A Ab	G	

(*tritone for F7.)

#2

			C B
Bb A	A Ab	G	

Tip: Once you have the changes down, try out some of the pedal point ideas you learned in the last chapter... for example suspending the first four bars, or playing suspended pedal tones under some of the ii V progressions.

Example:

G-7 | A-/D D7 | G-7 | D-7/G G7 |

C-7 | A-7/D D7 | G-7 | C-7/F F7 |

Bb-7/Eb Eb7 | A-7/D D7 | G-7 | Ab7 |

Softly As In A Morning Sunrise

Let's apply our knowledge to a minor key Jazz standard.   Have a listen to as many versions of SOFTLY as possible.

The A section is 8 bars and its pretty much nothing more than an 8 bar C- turnback...

How would you play it?

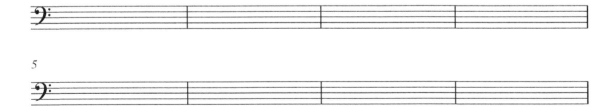

Next, listen to any version of SOFTLY Larry Young's version from **UNITY**...

Can you hear any interesting ideas? Try and write them down.

Note: Larry Young's concept of the A section is MODAL... his focus is on the key center.

Here's one line which is an amalgamation of a number of different patterns and strategies from various recordings...

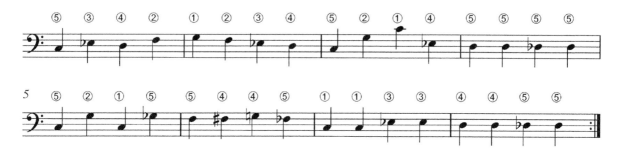

Softly isn't a modal tune per say, although the A section can most definitely be interpreted as thus.

Modal walking requires the imaginative ability to keep a line going and interesting for extended period of time. Of course, ostinato like lines are possible; however, being able to keep a walk like the one above going is essential, as an example, for hard bop type tunes that have to swing.

The best way to come up with ideas how to keep lines going is to study recordings, especially tunes like **IMPRESSIONS** and **SO WHAT.** – The big challenge is to create a walk that is smooth, flowing, driving and hypnotic, but isn't simply a monotonous I VI II V type line.

While the line above can help get you started, I must repeat over and over that nothing can replace listening to classic Jazz recordings and absorbing various concepts into your playing.

As for the line above, ii V is used to extend the I-7. There is also D-7/F to G7, with F used as an advice to walk up the V, before heading back to the one...

(Of course, don't forget about pedal point options too...!!!)

Once you can play tunes like this, the door is open for modal compositions where you have to stay in the same key center for extended periods of time. Some tunes to work on at this point include **SO WHAT**, **IMPRESSIONS** and **MOANIN'**. Since the chords and key centers aren't constantly changing these are pretty easy tune to play along with, so you might want to consider transcribing or studying the original versions.

Tip on Learning Tunes

When I was first starting to learn Jazz, the REAL BOOK was not available commercially. You would have to go to the "hipper" music shops and it would be sold behind the counter, so you'd have to ask for it and it wasn't cheap either. $35.00 was a lot of money back then, but once you had it, you could automatically have at your grip a great deal of the tunes that would allow you to play REAL Jazz gigs.

Today, anyway can pretty much get their hands on a sheet to almost any tune with a little clever goggling, and not only can the legal **REAL BOOK** be ordered anywhere, rivals exist (not to mention the Aebersold Play-a-long books!)

These resources are both a blessing – but also a curse.

Ideally speaking, the best way to learn tunes is by ear and transcription. After that sheets are o.k., but really you want to use them as a general guideline how to play the tune, relying on your own listening to figure out the "correct" changes. Unfortunately, many players of my generation simply haven't learned a lot of tunes by memory, instead we pull sheets. To the extent that we can pretty much play any tune put before us, not just the ones we know and rehearse. It is a step forward, but to the extent that we're not playing by ear and putting a lot of energy into reading sheets, its not so great.

My advice to musicians and music teachers alike is simple: Start your Jazz career by learning as many tunes as possible by memory. Certain tunes are easier to learn than others and once you have one set worth of musical material, its not hard to move on to another.

"SUNNY" and **"SOFTLY"** as an example are a few tunes that are pretty easy to memorize.

Sunny is pretty much just a progression that repeats with one variation in the end.

Softly is a C-minor turnback, with a I VI ii V I type bridge.

Let's learn another fairly simple one... **"SUGAR"**.

The original is by Stanley Turrnetine. Ron Carter is playing bass. Its definitely worth transcribing it.

Charles Earland also recorded a version in his later years...

Let's analyze the tune...

Sugar

Basically its nothing more than variations of a C- turnback for 8 bars. There are ii V prolongations and sometimes it hangs on the V, but you can get away with a lot if you do a lot of listening and playing-a-long with the tune. The most important thing to remember is that the last two bars have to walk up to the C- in the third measure...

D-7b5 | G7#5

The second part of the tune is sort of an extent end rundown.
It starts on C-7 but then goes Gb7 | F-7 | Eb7 | ...then back to the D-7 G7 walk up which concludes with Ab7 | G7

C-7 | Gb7 | F-7 | Eb7 |

D-7b5 | G7#5 | Ab7 | G7 |

Alright... let's review:

So we're hanging around for 8 bars, then doing a walk-up...

C up to Gb, F, Eb...

...then a 2 bar walk up as if we're going to C, but conclusion Ab7 | G7.

Based on this information, can you listen to a version of **SUGAR** (without referring to any sheet music), and write out the actual changes of the first 8 bars, and well as the second half of the tune???

Now, based on this information, can you play along with tune, playing your own bass line on the spot??? You don't have to play the exact same notes as the bass player. Just work on hanging with the band.

Once you've gotten the flow under your fingers, go back and listen to the recording. Are there any particular lines that interest you? Try to work it into your thing.

Of course there's no absolute one correct right or wrong bass line, but an important point to consider is the logic and flow of the bass line.

Harmonizing Tunes to enhance swing ("Summertime")

Let's have a look at a tune, and think of some ways of harmonizing it to improve the walk of the bass line. The tune I've chosen to undergo the makeover is **SUMMERTIME**.

Let's have a look at the changes...

A-7 | E7 | A-7 | A-7 |

D- | C-7 | B-7b5 | E7 |

A- | E7 | A-7 | G7 |

Came Fmaj | B-7b5 E7 | A-7 | E7 |

harmonic analysis (tip on lead sheet editing)

As bass players we don't simply play the notes written on paper, but we think about the harmonic structure of the tune and where things are going, then outline that form. This means that we have to be careful about simply playing the changes in a tune just because they're written on paper. For example, sometimes the changes include passing chords that are fine for pianists, or even horn players to blow on... but we don't really need to play them, so as a bass player, I often find myself editing lead sheets, sometimes mentally, mid tune.

When analyzing a lead sheet, the first thing I suggest is stripping it down to the bare basics. If you have a lead sheet to *SUMMERTIME*, please refer to it... Here's how I strip it down..

A-7			
D-7			
A-7			
Cmaj		A-7	

I-7			
IV-7			
I-7			
relative major		I-7	

Relative major and minor

This is basic music theory stuff that you need to know prior to studying Jazz. But just as a refresher, the relative major in a minor key can be found a minor third up. Hence, in A-, it would be C. These keys and scales have the same notes, but their harmonic tonality is different.

Chord Movement

So let's continue analyzing **SUMMERTIME**.

The first four bars are simply about prolongation. A common pattern in a Blues type progression is simply throwing in a V chord... so I-7 | V7 | I-7 | I-7 will suffice.

The tune then goes to IV-7 (much like a minor blues), but then it starts walking down to the one.

Then it goes to the IV-7 and starts walking back down to the I...

D D D D | C C C C | B B B B | Bb Bb Bb Bb | A....

(I've substituted E with its tri-tone Bb in order to make the walk more chromatic...)

Next, back to I-7 | V7 | I-7 -->

but in the next measure the tune goes to the relative major. In the last bar, the relative major is anticipated with the V chord leading to it...

Next it goes I IV then ii V back to the I-7....

Back to the I-7 | V7 | I-7 --> then a V chord targets the relative major...

and it cycles back to the minor by going I IV, then minor ii V back to the I-7

Remembering:

I-7

IV-7

I-7

relative minor | I-7

Make the tune a lot easier to memorize rather than playing it by reading each chord off the paper.

Now, let's look at the actual changes...

A-7	E7	A-7	A-7
D-7	C-7	B-7b5	E7alt
A-7	E7	A-7	G7
Cmaj Fmaj	B-7b5 E7	A-7	E7

We can also come up with clever subs and reharmonize any given tune in a variety of ways.

Some; however, may only be good for the solos as they'd interfere with the melody, others may require a bit of "banter" with the band before the performance...

A-7 F#7	B-7 E7	A-7 F#7	E-7b5 A7
D-7	C#-7 F#7	C-7 F7	B-7b5 E7
A-7 F#7	B-7 E7	A-7	D-7 G7
Cmaj Fmaj	B-7 E7	A-7 F#7	B-7 E7

Measure 1

Here, a prolongation device is required to keep the line swinging, so I use a the most basic of all prolongation devices, a turnback line. In the last bar; however, I need to get to D-7, so instead of playing A-7, I can play A7 or a ii V to the IV...

Measure 2

Bar 6 is an idea I came up with. The lead sheet I had gone to C-7, but I thought C7 sounded bluesier, but then I wondered what would happen if I played G-7 to C7 to keep it swinging. That was fine, but I noticed if I used the tri-tone sub, it connected with C-7 F7 which could lead to B-7 E7, hence a smooth transition to where I wanted to go.

Measure 3

Measure 3 includes the turnaround as a prolongation, then a ii V to the I (relative major 7).

Measure 4

Measure 4 in pretty easy: I IV progression followed by a turnback leading to the top.

This harmonization is not "right or wrong", its just my own concept for "SUMMERTIME" with the purpose of having a smoothly progressing hard bop type line.

Autumn Leaves

In order to play Autumn Leaves you need to be able to name the relative minor belonging to any key. The relative minor is located a minor third down from the root...

C D E F G A

      A B C D E F G

Next, create a bass line for the progression below, then learn it in all keys...

D-7 G7 | Cmaj7 Fmajor7 | F#-7b5 B7 | E-7

(!) Preparatory Exercise: In all keys play the ii V progression leading to the tonic, then the ii-7b5 V7 below it leading to the relative minor. ex. In G, A-7 D7 | Gmajor | F#-7b5 B7 | E-7

Now, let's try to memorize the tune.

The concept: ii V I progression to a major chord continuing to the major IV, followed by ii v to the relative minor.

For example, if you're in the key of G (REAL BOOK I key), you'd go ii | V | I | IV...

after the I you'd go ii V to the relative minor:

		G major	
		E minor	

You play the A section twice.

The BRIDGE reverses things...

You play ii V to the relative minor, then flip ii V to the major...

		E minor	
		Major	

The ending of the tune is ii V to the relative minor, there's an interesting walk down. I'll show you...

F#-7b5	B7b9	E-7 A7	D-7 G7
		E-7	

Where does the tune sound like its trying to go??? _____

But it doesn't go there... This is a type of *false cadence.*

Instead of going where you expect to, it goes back to the ii V leading to the minor chord...

(Don't forget that you can always chromatisize changes with tritones to make them flow more evenly... so you could go F# | F | E Eb | D Db

O.K. So let's review...

Two chords, a major chord, and its relative minor... So in G, Gmajor7 and E-7 are your "key centers" to remember.

Your key progressions are:

ii V I IV (major)

ii V I (minor)

That's the A section... Its all you have to know.

(*Work on the progression in all keys!)

Next, flip...

ii V to the minor I

ii V I major

Finally, the C section:

ii V I (minor) but continue to cycle down as if you were going to C...

repeat ii V I (minor)

That's it!!!

o.k. Based on this information, can you play the tune without looking at the changes?

Now, the challenge is to listen to a famous version. Jimmy Smith's version is played on the pedals as a ballad. Pedal playing isn't covered in our book, so let's have a listen, for example to Cannonball Adderley's version with the Miles Davis Quintet from *Something' Else*. This version begins with a simple A minor 6 figure played Ostinato...

At first the bass player is playing 2 beats to the bar. After the melody the bass begins walking. This is very conventional style of arranging.

Due to the laid back tempo of the tune its a great bass line for studying.

> **Don't forget, as an organist you are a bass player first and foremost, so studying legendary sessions with legendary bass players comes with the territory.**

Sample Bass Walk/ A Section / Autumn Leaves

This bass walk requires a lot of flow and dexterity. Its an example of a non-contained bass line that starts low, goes high, then swing back down. Many Jazz organists are afraid to do this, but if you watch real upright bass players when they're flowing, you'll see that they're usually not afraid to break out of the octave.

Practicing this line in different keys (with modified fingerings) can really get your line solid, so I suggest working on it as an etude starting off very slow at first and practicing it until you can play it in time without breaking the flow. After you've got it down, try to work out the rest of the tune. As a word of advice, it often helps to use contrasting counterpoint devices. For example, since the A section is being played very open, maybe contain the next section within the octave, or do a more root-fifth or chromatic prolongation type walk... or even reverse direction... This will keep your line interesting.

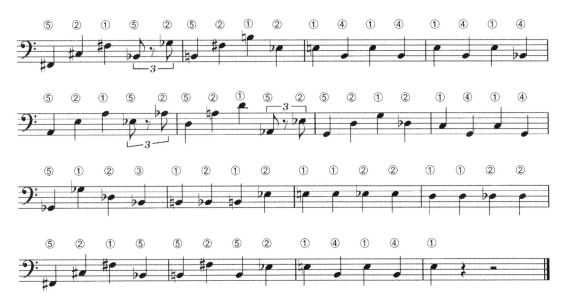

(*My interpretation of Autumn Leaves from the bridge to the end, strong root/fifth/octave type walk with occasional flips.)

7 RHYTHM CHANGES

After blues and minor blues, the most common song form all Jazz musicians are expected to know is rhythm changes. The basic concept is a I vi ii V turnback for 8 bars, which repeats itself, then a bridge which cycles back to the A section by going up a major third – but the 5th and 6th bars are usually fancied up, and the last two have to point either to the top or the bridge.

There are many variations of rhythm changes – Commonly played tunes to listen to include **I GOT RHYTHM, COTTON TAIL, LESTER LEAPS IN, MEET THE FLINTSTONES** and **OLEO**. Listen now then let's learn the form, then a stock model bass line.

Let's have a look at a simple version of the changes...

Bbmaj G7	C-7 F7	Bbmaj7 G7	C-7 F7
		Bbmaj G7	C-7 F7

A typical change for the fifth and 6th might be...

Bbmaj G7	C-7 F7	Bbmaj7 G7	C-7 F7
Bbmaj Bb7	Ebmajor Ab7	Bbmaj G7	C-7 F7

We've learned a lot about prolongations already... One way of keeping the tune from going back to the one would be by playing iii VI instead of I VI in the third bar.

Bbmaj G7	C-7 F7	*D-7 G7*	C-7 F7

| Bbmaj Bb7 | Ebmajor Ab7 | Bbmaj G7 | C-7 F7 |

I sometimes play a ii V to the I in the fifth and 6th bar...

| Bbmaj G7 | C-7 F7 | D-7 G7 | C-7 F7 |
| F-7 Bb7 | Ebmajor Ab7 | Bbmaj G7 | C-7 F7 |

And we can prolong the I chord in the 7th bar by replacing it with the iii...

| Bbmaj G7 | C-7 F7 | D-7 G7 | C-7 F7 |
| F-7 Bb7 | Ebmajor Ab7 | D-7 G7 | C-7 F7 |

Although an even more common strategy is...

| Bbmaj G7 | C-7 F7 | D-7 G7 | C-7 F7 |
| Bbmaj7 Bb7/D | Ebmajor Edim | D-7/F G7 | C-7 F7 |

Resulting in a bass walk as follows...

Bb Bb D D | Eb Eb E E | F F# G Db | C Gb F B |

This type of chromaticism can also be used over the I VI II V progression...

| Bbmaj Bdim | C-7 C#dim | D-7 Db7 | C-7 F7 |
| F-7 Bb7/E | Ebmajor D7 | D-7 Db7 | C-7 B7 |

If you purchase my book on harmony, you'll see how the B diminished voicing is the same chord shape as G7b9.

Bridge

For the bridge, as mentioned, we move up a major third, then cycle through a bunch of dominant 7ths until we get back up top. ..

D7	D7	G7	G7
C7	C7	C-7	F7

We can reharmonize this chromatically, of course...

D7	D7	Db7	Db7
C7	C7	B7	B7

Another trick to enhance the swing of a bass line is to replace the V with the ii...

A-7	D7	D-7	G7
G-7	C7	C-7	F7

Of course, the options don't end there... but let's stop for now and have a look at two stock model **Rhythm Changes** bass lines.

Stock Model Rhythm Changes Line

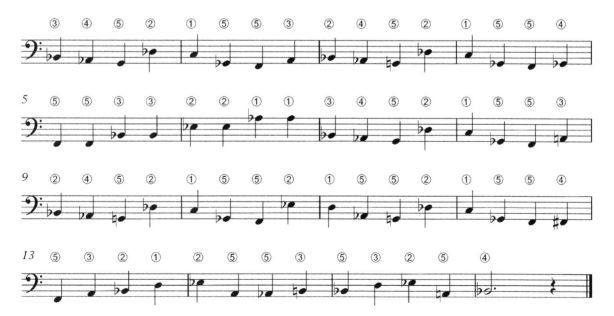

Here we have the A sections to rhythm changes in Bb.

The fingering breaks the rule we learned about roots being played with pinky and thumb, but in Jazz, no rule is firm. Let's look into the logic behind the line.

Hand Position Principles

The main idea behind the bass line above is to minimalize hand movement.

Try playing through it... How many hand positions can you find?

There are 3 at best, but basically, most of the A section is based on a single hand position.

The basic I vi ii V hand position, then the hand position for the Ebmajor run up.

Finally, the ending phrase.

They key point is that stable hand positions are essential for tunes with difficult changes, or that are played at rapid tempos. My own tendency as a player is to play a lot of "open position" type lines (lines that aren't necessarily confined to one octave); however, closed lines can offer more stability for rapid-fire walking under more complicated RH runs.

(!) Challenge: Recompose any of the lines you have learned so far in the book to confine the notes within about an octave.

The same bass figure is dealt with via two different fingerings: 3 4 5 2 to 2 4 5 2

Try getting the line flowing... The idea is to keep your hand in a stable position without having to do a lot of moving and crossing over.

Stock Model Bass Line: Rhythm Changes, The BRIDGE

This is a personal hook of mine....

8 MASTERING THE STANDARDS

Let's have a look at **ALL THE THINGS YOU ARE**, **I'll REMEMBER APRIL** then an even more difficult tune, **STELLA BY STARLIGHT.**

As a rule of thumb, to get a tune under your thumb, you want to analyze the following elements:

Key Center(s)/form of the tune

Where the changes are going

"signature changes" – type of resolutions

All The Things You Are

In the case of **ALL THE THINGS YOU ARE** we have an A A B A form...

According to the key signature we're in Ab... This means we need to be on the look out for chords like Abmajor, Dbmajor, F-7...

A general rule regarding how to analyze tunes is to make sure that you know the I, IV, ii V, iii VI on the spot to all keys... That should give a lot away... *(Below is not a chord progression, just a chart to remind you of the chord/roman numeral relationship.)*

I	IV	ii	V	iii	VI
Ab	Db	Bb	Eb	C-	F(7)

It also doesn't hurt to know as much as possible about the IV, V and the relative minor since tunes often modulate to these keys. (They don't always, but its going to happen a lot.)

Knowing this, in the case of **ALL THE THINGS YOU ARE**, a quick harmonic analysis of most of the A section shouldn't be so hard...

F-7	Bb-7	Ebmaj7	Ab7
Dbmaj7	D-7 G7	Cmaj7	Cmaj7

Initially speaking, we see a VI ii V I IV progression that resolves down a half step (via a ii V I progression) below the fourth..

This is a great walk to practice in all keys...

The walk continues a fifth away... with the Cmajor chord becoming minor and the pattern repeating itself...

C-7	F-7	Bb7	Ebmaj
Abmaj	A-7	D7	Gmajor

It should be apparent that this is the exact same pattern, only in another key (actually a fifth up.)

So this shouldn't be too hard to remember. We need two identical bass walks a fifth apart.

The bridge stays on the key we landed at for a measure then goes down to its relative minor...

A-7	D7	Gmaj	Gmaj
F#-7b5	B7	Emaj7	C7#9

The tune then concludes: VI ii iii VI ii V I

F-7	Bb-7	C-7	F7b9 (B dim7)
Bb-7	Eb7	Abmaj7	Abmaj7

In other words, its just walks home to the tonic.

So basically, even though the tune has 36 bars and some tricky resolutions, its not that hard after all...

--Its just two VI ii V I IV to a ii V a half step below progressions a fifth apart... (*When we move up a fifth, the tone is going to be the same... Cmaj7 → C-7)

--then it stays in that key (ii V to the I) and goes to that keys relative minor (ii-7b5 V I-7)

--then the tune begins an 8 bar walk down by fourths starting on the IV

So to practice this tune...

--Practice VI ii V I IV progressions walked up 1 bar per chord in all keys, then resolved down a half step with a ii V progression.

--Practice ii V to the major then ii V the relative minor in all keys.

--Practice an 8 bar walk down starting from the IV.

Once you have these three walks down, **ALL THE THINGS YOU ARE** should be simple, even at very fast tempos.

Of course, don't forget that you can also experiment with tri-tone substitution as well as pedal points...

For example, you can hang on the pedal point to create a sus feel on the bridge: Just hand on D for four bars, then go down a major third and play B!!!

Key Point:

Most Jazz standards consist of a limited number of either repeating or a certain distance a part progressions, so if you memorize the progressions then the concept of the tune, it shouldn't be that difficult to play.

Challenge: Leaf through the **REAL BOOK** and try to find as many standards as possible that can be memorized just by memorizing a few rules. (Also, don't forget many bebop tunes not found in the real book borrow the changes from classic standards... The more standards you know, the more "changes" you'll begin to recognize.)

I'll Remember April

I'll Remember April is a pretty high frequency Jazz session standard. Sonny Clark's version might be described as definitive for piano. Checking YOUTUBE, I found Johnny Hammond Smith playing it (with a bass player.) I know Groove Holmes did a great version too. Whatever the case, its definitely one of the top 100 standards all Jazz musicians are expected to know.

The key challenge in getting this tune down is the fact that its so darn long. Other than that, the logic isn't so difficult.

First, it starts out with four bars of a major chord, then four bars of the same chord memorized. *Not so hard...* Over the major chord I sometimes play pedal point D in alternating bars, and on minor, I alternate to C7. Some arrangements have these bars played Latin.)

This is the signature hook of the tune...

Gmaj7	Gmaj7/D	Gmaj7	Gmaj7/D
G-7	C7/G	G-7	C7/G

After this, the progression is pretty easy... basically, it goes ii-7b5 V iii VI7 ii V I... not so difficult!!!

A-7b5	D7	B-7b5	E7
A-7	D7	Gmaj	G7b9

This is the A section...

(!) Right away, listen to a few versions of the tune. Close the book, then try to play it... again, major/minor, ii V iii VI ii V I...

B Section

It then goes up a minor third, and pretty much repeats the same ii V I VI ii V I progression...

C-7	F7	Bbmaj	G-7
C-7	F7	Bbmaj7	Bb6

So, to practice this song you might want to play the tune over and over again nailing that ii V I VI ii V I progression a minor third apart.

Next thing that happens is sort of a slow walk down back home. --It goes back to the first ii V I (A-7 D7...), except in the next measure it continues down a minor third... then heads back to the tune's signature progression...

A-7	D7	Gmaj7	G6
F#-7	B7	Emaj	A-7 D7

The A Section pretty much repeats itself again.

Note: You want to break away from the written material as soon as possible. Work on one section at a time, then start putting them together. Switch over to any recorded version of the tune as soon as possible so you're not just memorizing a bass line, but rather training and using your ear.

Stella By Starlight

There are many tunes who's harmonic structure make them very easy to memorize. But what about more difficult ones?

Let's take **"Stella By Starlight"**. Many people consider it to be a difficult tune, but actually from a bass player's perspective, its quite simple.

Let's have a look at the first 8 bars for example:

E-7b5	A7b9	C-7	F7
F-7	Bb7	Ebmaj	Ab7

Skipping the first two bars, we see a bassline that's moving by fourths in two different types of ways.

One consists of two ii V progressions a fourth apart...   C F→ F Bb

The other bass movement purely by 4ths → F Bb Eb Ab

(The fourth walking then continues all the way up to Ab then climbs to Bb.)

ii V to the ii V modulating by fourths type line... (C, F, F, Bb)

Sequential fourth type line... (F, Bb, Eb, Ab)

If you have the two walks above under your fingers, playing STELLA is pretty easy once you get to the third bar. As you're doing the walk, remind yourself that you're climbing up a steep hill to Bb.

Once you get to the peak there are about 8 bars of total insanity unless you have a really good background in old school chord harmony.

Bbmaj | E-7b5 A7 | D-7 | Bb-7 Eb7 | Fmaj7...

Let me explain...

First, we're in the key of F... not Bb...

And here is how they might harmonize an F chord back in the day: (Play these chords back to back...)

A C D F
Bb Db E G
C D F A
Db E G Bb

Note: Db is part of the harmonic major scale, a major scale with a flattened 6th.

If you put the bass notes under it, it works...

(Bb) A C D F

(A) Bb Db E G

(D) C D F A

(Eb) Db E G Bb

(F) D F A C

Yet another way to remember the changes is an outline of the triad...

Bb D F which is IV (Bb) to to the *relative minor (D)* to the *tonic* (F)

D is targeted with a ii-7b5 V7, F with VII7.

review point: *name the tonic, IV and relative minor in all keys and play the STELLA progressions on the spot in each of them.*

o.k. I'll admit, those changes are a bit wacky, so its best to simply memorize the sound and feel in all keys.

Our changes so far...

E-7b5	A7b9	C-7	F7
F-7	Bb7	Ebmaj	Ab7
Bbmaj	E-7b5 A7	D-7	Bb-7 Eb7
Fmaj7			

There's one other alternative...

Bbmaj7 | A7 | D-7 | Eh7

So we see the F being targeted with a VII7 to the I type progression. *Very STELLA!!!*

Let's continue...

The tune returns to E-7b5 A7 then proceeds to walk by fourths; however, it has to get back to the tonic by the last bar. It gets to the tonic by creeping up from a whole step below... (VII7 I)

Fmaj	E-7b5 A7	A-7b5	D7
G7#5	C-7	Ab7	Bbmaj

STELLA ends with a simple one chord to the bar ii V cycle down to the tonic:

E-7b5	A7b9	D-7	G7
C-7	F7	Bbmaj	Bbmaj

Don't forget... through the magic of tritone substitution you can easily chromatisize the line...

E – Eb – D – Db – C – B - Bb

Practice Tips:

Stella has two hooks. One is the tendency of VII7s resolving to the I, the other is returning to E-7b5 A7.

As a practice tip, if a tune has an "unusual" (meaning new to you) progression, its good to practice it in all keys. For an organist, this would mean both the chord resolution and variations of the walk.

Let's review... Can you write out the changes by memory?

One exercise you can do when you have downtime and aren't by your instrument is to practice writing out the changes to various standards then in your head visualizing the bass line.

Also, note changes that epitomize the tune and try to recognize them when they occur in other tunes.

As an example, both **CHEROKEE** and **MY ROMANCE** have the VII7 to the I type progressions.

Cherokee starts on Bb, then goes F-7 | Bb7 | Ebmajor | Ab7 | Bbmajor.

My Romance B section goes Ebmajor | Ab7 Bbmajor7.

Sometimes you can come up with nicknames to chord progressions and use the nicknames to jostle your memory rather than memorizing the tune chord by chord (which is the wrong way to play since bass walking is about thinking about where you have to go, not merely playing chords.) If you weren't born with "perfect pitch", this is the secret to training your ear. You learn progressions and tunes, and recognize when you hear things that sound similar, then know to go back to those progressions.

9 3 / 4

Our book has covered the vast majority of what you need to know to survive a typical Jazz organ, even regular jam session – but not everything.

Please log on to my website for additional material, updates to this book as well as information on my upcoming books.

We'll close off with a quick lesson on ¾.

3/4

3/4 can be very tricky until you get used to it. Some commonly called 3/4 tunes are *"Someday My Prince Will Come"* , *"Alice In Wonderland"*, *"Up Jumped Spring"* and *"My Favorite Things"*.

The way I taught myself to play 3/4 was by displacing the 3 in 4/4... so, 1 2 3 4, becomes 1 2 +3...

Hence, your basic rhythmic motif is...

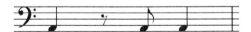

In 6/4, we need to double the pulse, but playing the same rhythm over and over might (in some cases) lead to a sense of monotony.   We can get around this by alternating between syncopated 3 and straight 3....

(Don't forget the importance of feeling the 2+5.) These are your "finger snap" beats...

If, for example, you break down 6/4 and ¾ times two, you have...

1 2 3 1 2 3

Which comes to...

1 2 3 4 5 6

But there are many ways you can feel the groove, for example you can tap your feet on the beat 6 times, or just on 1 3 and 5 while snapping your fingers on 2 and 5, or even 2 4 and 5.

Here's another variation...

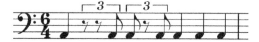

You may not be playing the notes exactly like this, but in your head, this would be how you're feeling the beat to get the feel.

Now, let's have a look at some sample bass approaches. The sample below is based on *"Alice In Wonderland"*.

If your 5 – 2 and 1 – 4 hand positions are solid, you should have no trouble playing these lines once you get the changes to the tune memorized.

On the other hand, here we have a bass line with a displaced fourth using a 1 5 1 (2 1 crossover) and 1 4 1 hand positions...

Eventually we might want to go for a "straight three" swing...

Eventually, your goal will be to have the same amount of effortless feel in your ¾ swing that you have in your 4/4 swing and to even be able to walk lines like...

To get a walk like this solid you'll need to master two things...

1.   Hand position and fingering

2.   The basic rhythmic motif of the line

The *rhythmic motif* of the line is...

As you listen to lot's of different Jazz recordings with organ as well as upright bass you can learn other rhythmic motifs then work out bass line to fit their structure.

For example, as a challenge, try to work out a bass line based on the motif below:

Rhythmic Motif

Rhythmic motifs last varying numbers of bars... 1, 2 and 4 most commonly. You can vastly widen your improvisational vocabulary by pinpointing them when you're hearing them, then learning how to "compose" and "hand position" them.

Challenge: Have a listen to any of your favorite recordings and transcribe the basic repetitive *rhythmic motif* you hear, then work out bass lines based on the patterns.

Suggested listening: Charles Earland's classic 1969 *"Black Talk"* album. (Its the one with *"More Today Than Yesterday")*

Why?: Hard grooving bass lines, but very patterned, so easy to study!!!

CONCLUSION

The first time I met John Patton, he sat me down at the organ and ordered me not to waste his time to start playing a blues. (See intro to this book.) I couldn't... or at least do much without stopping, restarting, speeding up, slowing down and being all over the place. John had me scoot off the bench and began an intense process of whipping me into shape. --At first, though, I had no idea what was going on...

Take for example, a 12 bar blues in F...

In this book, we learned something like this: F A Bb B | C D Eb E

but John would go...

C# C B | Bb A Bb B | C C# C B | C C B B...

Being able to catch up with his concept took time, but I was lucky because of that phone call with Hank Marr in which he told me the secret was a just needed a few lines going up and a few getting me down.

The next week I went to John's house and told him how much I liked Charles Earland's walk and he showed me that root fifth octave concept the mighty burner had going. Soon, almost over night things began to open up for me... and one thing lead to another and the next and the next.

From then on, I tried to pick the minds of the best organists I could find, many who sadly are no longer with us today, and the thing I learned time and time again is that a little knowledge is a dangerous thing. For example, I got to the point that I could walk some pretty mean bass lines, but I couldn't solo for the life of me. I talked about it to Lumpy King, one of Philly's old school Jazz organ greats. Lumpy said, "Just get your hand in position and play 3 5 7 9, that's all you gotta do." – "Play your chords!" John agreed. Suddenly, I went from not being able to play anything to being able to play something. It was a good start.

Then, I came across Bert Lignon's book on *Linear Harmony*... boom! A couple pages mixing *that* with *that* and I was on to the next level.

The late great Bobby Watley, who sadly died while I was writing this book heard the masters from my first CD and said, *"You gotta tap them pedals... otherwise your lines are gonna sound syrupy"* – Over the years, so many different players have showed me so many different things one utterance at a time.

In Jazz, we are always learning. Its not something we swallow all at once, or go to school for x number of years, get then carrying with us through life. Countless musicians (some pretty serious heavy weights) have told me, "I still can't play everything I hear!" –I remember asking Shirley Scott about that. I asked her if she had perfect pitch. She said no, and thank God. "If I could play everything I heard, I would have had no imperative to come up with my own style."

"Wow," I thought, *"There's hope for all of us."*

www.eddielandsberg.com

Printed in Great Britain
by Amazon